JESSICA RECTOR

Live Your
GREATEST
LIFE

DEDICATION

Dedicated to UB (1946-2006) for your laughter, understanding, and unwavering love. And to Tin and Skank, for always believing in me and for our friendships, "thank you" is never enough.

ACKNOWLEDGMENTS

The road I've traveled in getting to where I am now has been a great journey. Just like you, I've had my ups and downs, disappointments and triumphs, failures and successes. I've had to learn to accept myself for who I am and who I am not. In doing so, I've also learned to not only like myself but to love myself. I have struggled to find myself and what I truly want in life. With that has come the realization that if I can help ease the path for others, then that's my mission. I share with you my experiences and lessons with the hope that you will be open to learn something new and share it with others. I also wish for you the strength to disclose your trials and tribulations, as well as your joys and achievements with others, for you might be helping them in their journey.

There are many people who have helped me along the way and continue to do so. My two best friends, Skank and Tin, and I have lived in different states a lot longer than we lived in the same one, yet our friendships remain just as strong.

Tin, my best friend for seventeen years and counting—we've shared so many memorable times, and I'm blessed your first impression of me didn't stick too long. I love seeing how much we've grown not only as individuals but as friends. I know we will be little old lady best friends, still going to Chili's and playing Scrabble. Don't worry; I'll still beat you at it then, too.

Skank, you amaze me in your ability to provide such needed insight. You tell me the hard truth, yet have compassion when I need it. I cherish our friendship and recognize how far we have come in our lives.

Thank you both for your shoulders, love, and support, and most importantly for your understanding. Your listening skills are impeccable. You keep me grounded and sane, which I know may not always be easy. Thank you for never giving up on me. My world is so much grander for you being in it.

Ren, thank you for your honesty and humor. You make me laugh, give me encouragement, and provide truthful feedback. You three amazing individuals allow me to be me, and instead of finding fault in it, you love me unconditionally. Thank you for being my friends.

To my family...Dad, I know there have been times when you didn't understand what I was doing with my life. I hope this provides you with some assurance of my life's journey. All I ever wanted to do was to make you proud and for you to know I have succeeded by my definition. Thank you for realizing that you cannot hold me back from leaping, and I will either find my ground or fly.

Mom, we may disagree but we always find our way back. There is no one like you. You are the most giving and caring person I know. I am blessed to have you as my mom. Thank you for loving me and only wanting the best for me.

Doog, thank you for being my personal assistant. You helped me when I had no one else. Thank you for your wittiness. I can always count on you for a good laugh at the most random times. Thank you for caring, being creative, and knowing when things are sa-pi-tus.

Beast, I miss our conversations, sarcasm, and laughs. I miss you. I think of you often and want to build a future together. My life isn't the same without you.

Perg, I know no matter what, I can come to you. You will never judge, and will always encourage and support me. I know you will continue to help me in any way you can with my future endeavors. I can always count on you and your wife, who is just a blessing. Thank you for marrying well. More importantly, thank you to your wife for agreeing to marry my brother, because I lucked out in that deal.

My Deeds, you are the bright light in any dim day. I never knew the joy you would bring to my life. Thank you for always allowing me to be a kid again. Just the thought of you warms my heart.

My PGOL, from my first sight of you, our bond has only grown stronger throughout the years. Thank you for your husband. He is the person I most hoped you to be with. He is truly kind-hearted, and I know I don't have to worry about you (not that it will stop me). Thank you for the conversations, the Christmas light viewings, the puzzle doings, the Boo Boos visits, and all the moments in between. I cherish them all, as I do you. I know you "get" me without my having to explain it, as I do you. I will always be here for you.

To My Unborn Child, follow your heart. Never Settle. Explore. Discover. Dream. Live life to the fullest. Believe in yourself and all you have to offer this world. Be true to yourself. No matter where life takes you, I will love you and am proud to be your mom. Thank you for being exactly who you are.

My UB and Grandpa, I miss you guys still. Grandpa, you were truly interested in me and what I was doing, which made a huge impact on my life. I miss writing letters to you and receiving your responses. UB, you loved me, not because you were related to me, but because you wanted to. It made me feel safe and secure not following a traditional path in life, but instead following my heart and figuring out who I was. You taught me to be true to myself, and then helped me understand that when I am, people will like me. Thank you for all your love and support. I miss you.

This book is for all of you. It is for the ones who are insecure or don't understand who they are. It is for all of you who don't know how you got to where you are or don't know where to go. This book is for the ones who want to make a change but feel lost or confused. It's to you, your divine, wonderful, fabulous selves, who deserve better in your lives. It's for all the people out there who know they are great but haven't lived their greatness. You have no limitations! The world is your canvas. You can do and be anything! Ignite. Explore. Live. Now is the time to live your greatness. She is eager to be uncaged; allow her to spread her wings and soar. Let her out and FLY!

Thank you for your willingness to move forward in your life to be who you are meant to be and to reach your potential. Don't stop living your greatest life!

TABLE OF CONTENTS

love
generously

praise
loudly

live
fully

—Elias Portor

Introduction

There comes a time when all of us wonder, How did I get to this point in my life? Whether it's romantically, spiritually, emotionally, mentally, with your career or family, you wonder where along the journey you unwittingly decided to take one path over another. When did you let the life you've always dreamed of pass you by? When did you unknowingly let yourself become someone you don't recognize? How do you get her/him back? How do you find out who you really are?

Recognizing all of these is the beginning, and I applaud you for your willingness to see it and to know you need to do something about it. Often times the picture is so big that it overwhelms us, so we throw in the towel and think, I'll do it when…the kids are out of school…when I have more money…when I have another job…when my life is different…or better. Or it's just not the right time. Well, let's be honest, there never is a "right" time. Things will always arise, because that's how life is. Just when the one thing you've been waiting to happen actually occurs, something else comes up. That's just the way it goes.

Even when we know we want to make a change, we may not know where to start. Looking at all the things you have to do may boggle your mind, but don't let it engulf you. How do you begin when you don't know where to begin? When you don't know what questions to ask let alone how to find the answers or where to get the help you need?

Don't look at everything at once; if you do, it may crush you. By accomplishing your goals one at a time, your brain will be able to focus on the task at hand. Take it step by step. Put one foot in front of the other, then repeat this process over and over again. Before you know it, you will reach your first achievement, then the second. You will eventually be able to look back in amazement at all the progress you've made.

You can't afford to wait until life is perfect, because life will **never** be perfect. Don't waste another moment! Now is the time to live the life you've always dreamed of. NOW is the time to Live Your Greatest Life.

> # Now is the time to live your greatest life!

Slow down
Calm down
Don't worry
Don't hurry
Trust the process

—Alexandra Stoddard

CHAPTER 1: *Live Your Greatest Life*

What does 'Live Your Greatest Life' really mean? Better yet, what does it mean to you? How can you live your greatest life?

First let me encourage you that the greatest life you can live is not a perfect life. We know perfection in anything is not possible. It means living the life you want and that you've dreamed of having— the life you're meant to live.

Don't let anything stand in the way or hold you back from being exactly who you are meant to be. Many times our daily life gets in the way of the life we've envisioned for ourselves. Whether it is having a marriage partner, building a family together, or having a particular career, the things we were once certain we would have never materialize. Despite the disappointments you have endured, it's never too late to have the life you want.

You may spend $100 to get your hair done every six weeks or $130 on a pair of jeans. Entertainment or a meal out one night may cost $100-$125. You pay $70 for your kids to play soccer, have guitar lessons, and take ballet class for only a month. You'll take golf or dancing lessons for $80. But when it comes to doing a workshop or seminar to help yourself, you'll think twice about the $250, $100, or even the $75 it might cost to change your life.

Because things like hair, nails, food, and clothes are tangible objects, it's easier to justify spending money on them because you can see the immediate result or outcome, but with a seminar, you can't. But we all want to feel good on the inside. We can smile easier and enjoy life more fully when we aren't always saying, "I hate this job," or "When am I going to find the love of my life?" When we feel complete, it radiates to our outside and enhances our appearance. When we don't, no amount of retail therapy will make up for this inner lack.

Think about your dilemmas. Is it your job? Do you want to go back to school? Do you long to discover your passion? Do you hope to find the person of your dreams? Do you need to get out of debt? Do you desire to travel? Or maybe you want to grow your business?

Most often, the things we want to change are things on the inside, yet we are hesitant to spend money to make those changes. We don't mind spending money on outside things, such as activities, entertainment, and dining out. Why do we hesitate to do something that will help us inside and allow us to be who we are meant to be, and help us to have a better future? Those should be our priorities, not what restaurant we want to eat at tonight or the location of our seats in the stadium.

So, when you have a chance to help yourself reach your potential, don't even think about it. Jump at the opportunity. A personal session with a life coach, workshops, seminars, conferences, and conventions to help you better yourself are all worthwhile endeavors. People learn in different ways, so it's good to immerse yourself in a variety of methods to find out which way is best for you. Get your company to hire a speaker to increase sales, grow the business, or to help you learn about you, as that ultimately benefits the business, too.

When there are unresolved issues in your professional or personal life, these affect other areas of your life as well. As much as bosses say, "Leave your personal problems at the door," the reality is it doesn't usually happen.

I want you to become the person you are meant to be and to reach your potential. When you look back on your life, you will have no regrets and know you've lived a good life. You will have lived the life you have always thought about and wanted to live. You don't want to look back and wonder why you did or didn't do something, or what your contribution to the world could have been. You want to remember all you've done to be your greatest self. You want to be proud of your milestones and who you are.

This book is about you...about being your authentic self in every way possible. It's about you living your dream. We can't do everything on our own, no matter how much we think we can or how much we want to. We just can't. It's not possible. You don't have all the answers, and there is nothing wrong with getting input from someone who can help you receive answers and solve your dilemmas.

A life coach, just like a coach in sports, will help you attain a better life in all aspects of your life. Workshops and seminars will provide you with a ton of information. Ideally, when you get home, you will be thinking a lot about your life, where it is and where you want it to be. Conferences have sessions presented by many different speakers, and you can choose which sessions to attend based on your life goals at the time of the conferences. Conventions are great for businesses, industries, and professionals to learn more about the professional world.

If you have to pay $100, $300, or $1000 to participate in these, isn't it worth it if you are going to change your life as a result? Most of us spend more than that in a year on entertainment, shopping or going to the salon. If a few hundred dollars is the price you pay for changing your life, you are getting a real bargain. It is like going to a garage sale and getting an antique worth thousands, and you paid $2 for it. Wouldn't you leap over anything to get to that item before anyone else could? That's how you should be thinking of your life: If someone presents you with an opportunity to change your life for the better, do whatever it takes to make it happen.

All those other things you spend money on are temporary solutions (eating, concerts, clothes, sports or dance lessons); transforming your life is permanent. The money you are willing to spend on those things should transfer over to your desire to change your life. Once you do that, your life will never be the same, and who knows—you will probably get the money you invested in your life back ten or one hundred fold. Then you will know the investment was well worth it. If you think eating at a restaurant and attending live sporting events and concerts are worth the money, don't you think you are worth at least that same investment? You are well worth that and more!

> # Prioritize yourself.
> # Work on the inside before
> # looking to the outside.

The Process

When you go into a large grocery store to get milk, you may think you are going to run in and out in ten, maybe fifteen minutes. Then you pick up orange juice, bread, ice cream, and maybe some cookies along the way. If you are feeling really daring, you might grab some fresh fruit too. It takes you fifteen minutes just to get to the checkout line.

Patience may not be your strength, so you get in the shortest line. You wait and wait and then notice the line next to you is moving faster than the line you are in, so you jump to that line. Little do you know that although there is only one person in front of you, she needs a price check, which means the manager has to be called over. Then she can't find her wallet, and when she finally does, her card doesn't work in the machine. You glance at your original line and realize that if you had just stayed there, you would have been gone already and on your way home. But your impatience got the best of you. Instead of running in and out in fifteen minutes, you are out in more like forty-five minutes.

You always think if you just have to get one or two things at the store, you can run in and out, and then somehow you get stuck in there, through no fault of your own, for what seems like forever. But yet it never keeps you from expecting it to change the next time around.

If you have a child with you, tack on another hour. Actually, with a kid in tow, there is no such thing as running in and out of anywhere. Whatever you think is going to take you thirty minutes is really going to take you an hour and thirty minutes.

I don't want you to think of this book as a running-in-and-out-of-the-grocery-store kind of experience where you can hopefully do it all in fifteen minutes and things will go exactly as you plan. If you want a quick fix, then this process won't work. There is no fast, easy way to live your greatest life. If there were, you would probably already be doing it.

It's a life change. It's not an instant process. There is no fairy princess who will come along, wave a magic wand, and make all your troubles go away.

Whenever any of us starts something new, we're never good at it. There is always a learning curve. Think of what it was like when you became a parent, started driving, or began playing a sport. You weren't great at first. It took time and practice to excel and achieve mastery. It's no different with living your greatest life. It's a process. And it takes time. It may take you months or a year. There is no deadline for you to meet. There is no pressure to reach a goal by a certain date. You can't and shouldn't rush the process. You'll be doing a real disservice to yourself if you do, and that won't help in the long run. As long as you have breath in your body, there will always be new goals to reach and new ways to fulfill your purpose in life.

We come to these realizations at different stages and at varying rates. Don't compare yourself to someone else. If you and a loved one are focused on improving your lives at the same time, I encourage you to talk about it with each other. Although it may be difficult, don't make comparisons. Each of you will be at a slightly different stage (emotionally, physically, mentally, psychologically, socially, economically) than the other. When one of those stages varies, it affects everything else. No two people are the same. Even if you are a twin, you won't have the same life experiences your twin has. Therefore, it's impossible to compare yourself and your discovery process with anyone else. Some parts will be easier or more difficult for you than they will be for others. And that's okay, because that's exactly as it should be.

It's all about the work you put in to get the results you want. You need to make a commitment to yourself. Be willing to dig. Be willing to open yourself up. Be willing to be vulnerable. You must be 100% honest with yourself. Honestly is the only way you will achieve success. We all have things about ourselves that we don't much care for, or things we want to work on or change. If you are not honest and true to yourself about what those things are, then this process will not work. If you are not going to give this journey all of yourself, then you will remain in the same situation you are in right now. And you don't want that. That's the reason you are reading this book in the first place. I have full faith in you being honest with yourself. You've already started by taking the first step—realizing you want to make a change. Now, it comes down to your dedication and motivation to live your greatest life. It's a long distance marathon, not a sprint. So, sit back, relax, and enjoy the process.

> # Be completely honest with yourself. It's the only way this process will work.

What You Need to Know

One of my goals is to get you to think. Think about your life; really think hard and deep. Don't scratch the surface. Dig down and think why you are where you are right now. What decisions have you made that steered you away from your true path? What are you not doing that you should be doing? Why aren't you doing it? Think about you. What do you want? What do you envision for your life? What do you think and feel? Be completely honest with yourself. Don't hold back. If you do, the only person it will hurt is you.

I'm here to help you in any way I can. But one thing I won't do is tell you what you want to hear. I'm not here for that. If you are like most people, your spouse, co-workers, and friends do that already because they don't want to hurt your feelings. Well, I'm here to tell you the truth, because I've been where you are. I know what it's like to be in a lifeless relationship, a dreadful job, or struggling with finances. We are in this together. I hope you've gotten to a point in your life where you are open and willing to hear the truth. When it's difficult to face something, the last thing you want is for someone to be harsh and mean about it.

I want to help you. If that means telling you what the most important people in your life are not willing to tell you, then that's exactly what I'll do. If those "important" people aren't telling you what you need to hear, maybe you should re-evaluate those relationships and ask yourself, "Why are these people significant in my life if they allow me to think/believe/do/say_____ (fill in the blank)?" You need people in your life who will be completely honest with you.

I will tell you what you need to hear, not what you want to hear. They are two very different things. You are already on the right track by knowing you need to take the steps to live your greatest life. I'm blessed our paths have crossed. Now, you are ready to begin.

> # We are in this together. I'm here for you, plain and simple.

You are NOT alone.

—Anonymous

CHAPTER 2: *First Things First*

Yes, you've taken the first step. You were honest with yourself about needing to make a change. That's the beginning, and I'm proud of you for recognizing things are not the way you want them to be in your life.

To help you remember the key points in this chapter, think of the acronym **RISE**. It stands for Realize, Imagine, Soar, Empower.

Realize

The first thing you need to do is *realize* that things are not quite right or they are not working for you. You then *recognize* something needs to change and you are willing to make that change. You just need help in doing so.

You've acknowledged to yourself (by reading this book) that a change is in order. Now you need to verbally express the specific change that you want. You need to say this aloud: "I need to change _____." You fill in the blank.

It goes something like these:

"I'm not happy with my marriage. I need to have better communication. In order to do that, I need to be more open. What is keeping me from being more open?"

"I want to find my soul mate. I don't know where to find him. I need help in knowing where to look."

"I don't like my job. I want a career change and to find my passion. How do I do that? Where do I start?"

It begins by establishing what you are not happy with in your life, but it's important to be specific. The more specific you are the better. It's not going to help you to just say you are not happy. You need to get to the root or source of that unhappiness. Once you find that, ask yourself what it is going to take to fix it. You may not know the means or tools of improving it, but you have an idea of what could make it better. The above examples demonstrate how someone wants to change her life. She may not know where to start, or what she needs in order to resolve her dilemma, but she knows what the issue is. You know you need a change; now identify your specific issue.

Once you've done that, you need to do three things to make it real. These three are essential. First, think of what you need to change. Then, when you are alone, say it aloud to just yourself. This is important! Once you say it aloud to yourself, you can't live in denial anymore. Finally, admit it to someone else. That is the hardest thing to do because we all want to be accepted, liked, and loved. No matter how well we know the person we're telling, we still don't want her to think we are a loser, or that we're thinking negatively.

When Donna's friend picked her up for shopping one afternoon, Donna never could have predicted how the day would end. Donna had a few drinks for lunch, and her friend confronted her about it. After denying it several times, Donna finally admitted to drinking her lunch. Donna could no longer hold back everything that she had kept bottled up inside her for so many years, and she broke down and poured out her heart to her friend. At thirty-five, Donna was depressed about how her life had turned out. She never thought she would be this person—not married, no kids, and only a few friends—by the time she had reached this age. She craved a better social life. She wanted to feel like she fit in, but she didn't know how. So she had turned to alcohol for comfort.

Donna was drinking every night and sometimes even during the day. She knew it wasn't good for her, but she was lonely and miserable. She didn't know what else to do. She often found herself wondering, *How do you make friends?* She felt lost and scared. No one had ever helped her understand what happens when we struggle with low self-esteem, nor had anyone shown her how to increase her self-confidence.

No one ever teaches us that in school.

Donna had never revealed any of this to another person before that day. She was terrified of what someone else would say; she was certain that everyone would be judgmental and show no compassion for her. She didn't want anyone to think, *She is so pathetic. What a loser!* So she had kept it inside, never releasing the hurt and pain.

Donna's friend listened and understood. She comforted and supported Donna during this time and provided her with ideas to make the changes she wanted. Once Donna told her friend her feelings, she freed herself from all the bottled-up emotions that had taken over her life and kept her trapped. She felt liberated. She was alive.

No matter how much Donna knew deep down that her friend would accept her and love her, it was the actual telling of these painful secrets that was causing her such agony. Donna dreaded her friend's response as though it would change the rest of her life. No matter how "sure" she was of the answer, though, she was still only 99.9999 percent sure. The .0001 percent of doubt was engulfing her like a tidal wave, but it didn't drown her. Once Donna shared her heart with her friend and got her supportive response, all was well—just like it will be when you tell your friend.

Admitting our pain to someone else allows it to be real, something that can't be taken back. Have you seen the movie "When Harry Met Sally?" At the beginning of the movie, they are in a diner on their road trip to New York, where Harry tells Sally that she's an attractive woman. Sally says it's a "come on" and he's hitting on her, but he's going out with her girlfriend, Amanda. He tells Sally that his compliment was not a come-on, but that he will take it back anyway. She says, "Well, it's already out there and you can't take it back."

Likewise, once you verbalize something to someone else, it's out there. You can't act like it doesn't exist. You said it to the world; now own it. Be proud of it. Tell someone your pain and hurt. We all have flaws, and one day you'll be on the receiving end of your friend's acknowledgement of her pain or an issue she's struggling with.

> # REALIZE your pain to yourself, verbally, and then to someone else.

Imagine

After the realizing step, the next step is to *imagine* what your future can hold. You need to think about all the things that can become your reality. All the things you have longed for but somehow haven't allowed yourself to have are still attainable.

Imagine finding the love of your life, pursuing your dream career, or maintaining your finances successfully. When one thing changes in your life, think of the effect that will have on every other aspect of your life. It's not just about making one part of your life better. It will alter everything in your life and make it greater, grander, and happier. It will allow you to see the possibilities that can exist in your life.

Don't just think you can have "it," whatever "it" may be. When you imagine it, live it down to your core. Use all your senses. What will you see when you get it? Lights flashing? Where will you be? Are you inside? Outside? Standing? Sitting? What's your location? What colors are present? What time of day is it? Who else is with you?

What do you hear? Are people cheering you on? Is it silent? Is there laugher? Are cars driving by? Is a server taking your order? Are birds chirping in the background? Are horns honking? Can you hear water trickling from a fountain?

What do you taste? Did you just eat chocolate? Maybe you're in the middle of a jog. Are you drinking water? Is your mouth dry because you're out of breath? Are you eating dinner? If so, is it sushi? Steak? Did you just fall on your face or is it the sweet taste of success?

What do you smell? Flowers? Gasoline? Freshly cut grass? Did you just buy a new car, and the new car aroma still lingers? Does it smell like it's going to rain?

What do you feel? What is at your fingertips? Are you lying on a leather couch? Are you walking along a shag carpet? Is your face leaning into your hands?

What are your feelings? Victory? Relief? Astonishment? Glory? Bravery? Strength? Unbelief? Do you feel like you're going to faint?

When you put your full heart and soul into imagining what your world will be like once you have what your heart desires, then—and only then—will you start to really believe you can achieve it. Picture yourself in the exact place and time it will happen. See yourself truly there, and it will become a reality. You can't just halfway imagine it or think, *Yeah that would be really nice to have.* You have to fully commit yourself to making it happen and then living it, because it is possible. Believe you deserve it. Believe it can and will happen to you. Once you wrap your mind and heart around it, it will be your reality...your life!

Use all five senses to IMAGINE yourself having "it"— whatever it is you desire.

Soar

When you use all five senses to immerse yourself fully into achieving what you want, your spirit will find its wings. An amazing transformation takes place once you are able to picture yourself getting what it is you desire. Your mind focuses, your perception alters, your attitude is enhanced. You realize what matters and what is not important. When you've wasted so much time worrying about issues, people, and situations that don't mean anything, you can truly see what your life holds and what is in store for you when you free yourself from those empty concerns.

You will finally know what *you* are seeking—not what someone else thinks is important, what he thinks you should be doing, or whom she thinks you should be, but what you want. You might not have any idea how to go about getting it, but when you know what you want, you are better equipped to discover what you need to get it, and you're able to recognize it when you do.

Your spirit has been longing to fly. It wants to soar and allow you to be who you are meant to be. When you eliminate all the unwanted people and unnecessary things from your life and spend more time focusing on and working toward your goals, your spirit soars. The higher your soul flies, the more you will want it to continue.

It's a challenge, because you might feel pulled in different directions by your responsibilities and priorities. I'm not telling you to abandon them but you owe it to yourself to take the time to improve yourself. Without first working on you, there's no way you can make an authentic contribution to others' lives. How can you offer yourself, whether it's through advice, work, love, or being an example, if you're not willing to walk the talk, to give to yourself what you offer to others? How can you expect and want others to follow their dreams, find their love, and discover their passion if you aren't willing to do the same? If you are supporting and encouraging others but you're not doing this for yourself, you're living a lie. No one wants to live a lie. But that's exactly what you're doing. If you expect others to realize their potential and become who they truly are, then you have to be willing to put yourself out there to do the same.

It's not about making other people happy. We can't control others' feelings. If we are happy within ourselves, though, others will feel it. Give yourself what you need, and you will be able to help others get what they need.

When your mind, heart, and spirit come together in a balanced state—when you are fixed on a goal and are able to achieve it with great success, and I know you will—you will soar. Your wings will be so grand, you won't know what to do with yourself, and that, my friend, is an amazing feeling. That is possible for you—to feel...to be...to soar.

> # Focus on yourself, and your wings will allow you to SOAR.

Empower

When you've gone through years of insecurity and self-doubt, it's difficult to see your worth. It's hard to imagine that you can reach a goal you've set for yourself. When someone tells you something negative often enough, you start to believe it. You allow it to become part of you. You buy into the "I'm not good enough" mentality. I'm not _____(smart, pretty, thin, funny, successful, etc.) enough. You eventually think you won't be, do or get what you want, and you're convinced that you definitely don't deserve it.

Believing in yourself is a mindset. Who has control over your mind? Only YOU do! No one controls the most powerful part of you but you. Allowing someone else to have that power over you is detrimental to your well-being. It will only bring you down and keep you from being who you are meant to be.

You can't go through life comparing yourself to other people. There will always be someone smarter, prettier, thinner, funnier, and more successful than you. Someone will always have more; that's just life. If you constantly compare yourself to others, you will never measure up. Furthermore, for every way that you think you aren't as good as someone else, you exceed them in other aspects. Maybe they are smarter but you are kinder, more giving, loving, honest, and respected. It's not about comparisons. It's about knowing what can't be changed, and changing the things you can change. You have the power to change. You just have to take the steps to do it and make sure you follow through.

Believing you can and will achieve anything you set your mind to do is all about changing how you think. You can't allow anyone or anything to win control and overpower you, because you have all the power and strength necessary to accomplish great things in life. You have everything within you. Everything is already there. You just have to feel it, know it, and believe it.

When you believe in yourself, you empower yourself to not only achieve this one thing but to accomplish so much more. When you empower yourself, you empower your household, children, peers, family, and friends. Your empowerment will be felt by everyone around you, and they will be empowered to achieve greatness in their own lives. When you empower yourself, you empower the world.

> # When you believe in yourself, not only do you EMPOWER yourself. You EMPOWER others too!

Begin

Anywhere.

—John Cage

CHAPTER 3: What It Means to RISE

RISE is more than just a verb. It's more than an action. It's a stance. RISE above the voices, experiences, and obstacles...the things and people that keep you down. RISE above them. Let them know they don't have control over you or your emotions and that you are no longer allowing them into your life.

We all have responsibilities. We have to work to pay the bills or take care of our house and kids. That doesn't mean we have to hate every minute of our job or that we can't spend time on ourselves.

If you invest in you, you will create the foundation to RISE.

Limitations shouldn't exist. They are there to tell you that you can only go so far, and that's not true. When your heart and mind are set on something, you have the power to achieve it. No one can take that away from you. RISE beyond the limitations and expectations others put on you. RISE above the ones you put on yourself. RISE to the stars!

When a co-worker or your boss treats you unjustly, do you let them continue on that path or do you stand up for yourself? You know in your heart what is right. Do you speak it or continue to take the abuse? RISE for what you believe in.

If a child is being bullied in front of you, do you ignore it and keep walking, thinking, *It's none of my business*? Or do you take the time to get involved? What if you knew ahead of time that if you interceded on that child's behalf, it could save the child's life? Would you then get involved? RISE up for others.

Rising up for yourself and others doesn't constitute being mean, rude, or hurtful. Take a stance without disrespecting yourself or others. But RISE up for what you believe!

Are you doing what you want to be doing? Are you living the way you want to live? Many of us don't understand how our life came to be what it is. People want to make a change in their lives, but since they don't know how or where to start, they don't bother. They give up.

You have to be willing to take the first step and have the passion to follow through. As much as I want you to want this for yourself, I can't make you do it. I can't teach you to be passionate about yourself. I can't give you that hunger to want a better future. When *you* are passionate and hungry, you will stop at nothing to make it happen. I can put tools, techniques, and steps in front of you, but it takes you and only you to start. And it takes you again to have the drive to follow through. When you are hungry, you will fight for it...fight for the change you want...fight for the life you want... fight for the *you* that you want.

Once you do that, you will be amazed to see how many opportunities present themselves to you, and when that happens, your world will change. It may be difficult for you to imagine finally having the job, marriage, respect, love, or life that you want, but it's all possible. RISE to know it's possible.

RISE—Realize Imagine Soar Empower. You can do it. You can RISE. It all begins with you.

When you choose to RISE, life is your canvas. When you choose to RISE, the world is at your fingertips. When you choose to RISE, opportunities you never imagined present themselves. When you choose to RISE, everything and anything is possible. When you choose to RISE, you finally become you...the person you were always meant to be. It's your choice. RISE is not just a verb or action; it's a stance. Take your stance today and RISE!

RISE is a stance! It all begins with you.

LIFE ISN'T ABOUT FINDING YOURSELF.

LIFE IS ABOUT CREATING YOURSELF.

—UNKNOWN

STEP 1: DISCOVERING WHO YOU ARE

CHAPTER 4: *Who Are You?*

When someone asks who you are, how do you answer? Do you say you're a mother of three, a spouse, or that you work for Joe Smith Company? If so, that doesn't really tell anyone who you are. Those things don't define us, yet many of us respond with those kinds of answers.

Have you lost yourself somewhere between taking care of three kids under the age of five and making sure the house looks decent? Have you lost yourself in the fifty-hour-a-week-job you can't stand? Have you been married for twenty years and become just like your spouse, burying who you really are? Are you divorced, with no kids at home, and often feel as though you don't know what to do with yourself? Do you sit on the bathroom floor at night and quietly cry to yourself because you feel a hole inside your chest that's swallowing you up? Where did you go? How do you find yourself again?

It's hard to start when you don't know where to start. You have nothing to focus on because you feel like everything is in shambles. Or you delude yourself into believing nothing is wrong; everything is fine. The more you say it, the more you believe it until one day you feel everything come crashing down. There may be one part of your life that you've wanted to work on, but other things—more important things, or so you told yourself—came up, and so you decided it could wait. You have been willing to wait to work on you. How many times have you done that? How often do you put yourself on the back burner because something or someone else is more important?

Stop putting it off. Stop making excuses! You're not benefiting anyone, especially not yourself. If you aren't taking care of yourself and your needs, you can't fully take care of someone else. No matter how much you want to believe otherwise, it just simply isn't true.

I know you are reading this book because you recognize you need to do something to make a change in your life. I want to encourage you to follow through. Reading this book is only part of the journey. You will need to work through the steps covered in this book and make sure you give yourself adequate time to internalize the process. And by 'adequate time', I mean enough time to work through each stage at a pace that is comfortable for you, but not so much time that you forget about putting these steps to work for you, and ultimately, forgetting them altogether. You have to decide what is best for you, but don't quit. Don't give up.

Some steps may be more difficult than others, but persevere through them anyway. You are stronger than you think. I know you can do it. Keep at it, keep moving forward, and never ever give up! You are worth fighting for. Your self-worth is of the utmost importance, so the struggle will merit the prize. The only person who can make the change is you. The only person who will put in the work is you. The only person who will follow through is you. The only person who has to motivate you is you. YOU are the sole person responsible for YOU. YOU are the sole person responsible for making the change to live your greatest life!

Gone are the times of blaming other people for where you are in your life or for what hasn't worked the way you wanted it to. Maybe your dad wasn't in your life or your spouse didn't love you enough. Your mom didn't give you enough attention or she gave you too much. Despite the original source of your pain, stop blaming others for the way your life has turned out. The days have passed when you have had other things to do or other people who needed you. I'm not saying they won't need you again; rather, their needing you is not more important than you needing yourself. You are responsible for your own life. No one made your life what it is or what it isn't.

YOU are RESPONSIBLE for YOU. No one else is...JUST YOU! And now is the time to change your life to be the greatest it can be!

> When someone asks, "Who are you," how do you answer?

I beg you...to have **patience** with everything unresolved in your heart and try to **love** the questions themselves as if they were locked rooms or books written in a very foreign language. Don't search for the answers, which could not be given to you now, because you would not be able to live them. And the point is, to live **everything**. Live the questions now. Perhaps then, someday far in the future, you will gradually, without even noticing it, **live** your way into the answer...

—Rainer Maria Rilke

CHAPTER 5: *Ask Yourself the Hard Questions*

The hard questions are the ones that still linger and weigh in your mind or on your heart in some way. There isn't one generic question that everyone needs to ask herself. You have to be willing to look inside yourself to figure out what the hard questions are for you.

Taylor was on his way to achieving a professional basketball career, but he injured his knee and had to have surgery as a result. His career was over before it even started. So I asked him, if he could play one game of pro ball or never play another game of ball in his life, which would he choose?

Susie didn't have a good relationship with her dad growing up. As an adult, she decided to put the past behind her and start from the present to build a relationship with him. Her dad unexpectedly died before she had a chance to do that. So, I asked her, if she could have one more conversation or one more day with him, what would she say? Where would she go? What would she do?

Asking yourself the hard questions will help you deal with any unresolved feelings you have about certain situations, experiences, or people. It will help you mend and move past those things you have not released. They are preventing you from taking the next step. When you let them go, you will be able to move on and move forward with your life. It's not about forgetting them. It's about coming to a resolution that fills that vacancy, disappointment, or sadness and allows you to recover. Living in a state of resentment or loss will never allow you to find and be your true self.

Finding the hard questions to ask yourself may be easier than answering them. It may take you an hour, a day, or a week to get to the root of your pain and thus find the answers. Be encouraged: You have all the answers within you, but it's not a sprint. Take your time. Don't rush the answers; find your way to them.

At one point or another in our lives, we have all asked ourselves the "Why me?" question, but this is a fruitless exercise because we will never know the answer. So, whatever hard questions you are asking yourself, it serves no purpose to ask "Why me?" It doesn't matter "why you," Because it isn't just you. Everyone struggles with that question. All you need to do is acknowledge that it is what it is, and then decide what you are going to do about it. Everything is a matter of choice. You may not like your choices, but you ALWAYS have a choice. So instead of asking, "Why me?" you can always flip it and ask, "Why not me?"

You have to dive inside yourself to find your hard questions. No two people will have the same ones. You have to be able and willing to dig deep to figure them out. Before you go any further in the process, look inside your heart and find out what has yet to be resolved, and then find its solution.

Don't rush to the answers.
Find your way to them.

Go for long walks,
indulge in hot baths.
Question your assumptions,
be *kind* to yourself,
live for the moment,
loosen up, *scream*,
curse the world,
count your blessings,
just let *go*, just *be*.

—Carol Shields

CHAPTER 6: *Would You Rather...*

Lacy, my best friend, and I have known each other for seventeen years. Several years after we met, we made up this game called "Would You Rather" (now a board game, wish we would have thought to create that) where we would ask each other random, far-fetched questions such as, "Would you rather have your lip or eyebrow pierced?" We would ask each other any question that came to our minds. The great thing about this game is that you learn about the other person, but you also learn so much about yourself... things you never thought about before.

If you're scared of heights, would you rather go skydiving or never try another new thing again in your entire life? Before you answer the question too quickly, think about it. Suppose you are really terrified of heights, but you have the choice to either jump out of a plane or never try another new thing again. That means no new food, restaurant, or experience. If you have never taken your kids to Disneyland, you'll never be able to take them. If you have never taken someone you love to the city of love, Paris, you'll never be able to take him/her. In other words, you wouldn't be able to try anything new again, ever. What would you rather do?

Now imagine you are given a million dollars. You can keep the million or give $10,000 dollars away to a hundred people. Which would you rather do?

Let your imagination go wild with the questions. The more you release it and give it permission to ask the craziest questions, the more you will learn about yourself. Nothing is off limits, because don't you want to know everything you can about yourself? There are no right or wrong answers, only the truth. Give yourself permission to be fully honest, even if it's not the answer you want to discover about yourself, the choice that would be the most popular, or the one that seems better. Give your full and honest answer, and accept what it is.

In the first example, if you chose never to try another new thing again, then you need to ask yourself why you would not face your fear of heights. Why do you want your fear to continue to control you? What are you really afraid of? If you chose to overcome your fear and go skydiving, what does that say about you? If you've had the opportunity to do it, why haven't you? What's stopping you from confronting that fear now?

In the other example, if you chose to keep the million dollars, what would you do with the money? Are you greedy? Does money define you? Do you think money implies status? How much status do you place on your life? If you said you would give the money away, what were your motives? Are you hoping to get something in return, or would it be a freely given gift?

It's difficult to admit answers that you may not like or that others may view as the "wrong" answers, but there are no right or wrong answers. They are there for you to learn more about you. The more truth to your answers, the more you can uncover about yourself.

The "Would You Rather" game helps you discover a lot about yourself, but you also should be willing to dig deeper to find out what your answers reveal about you, your situation, your life, and your relationships. When you are willing to delve into the answers, you will discover what you like, dislike, value, believe, will stand up for, tolerate, who matters, and who isn't important to you. All of this information can play a vital role in your life. So grab your best friend or do it alone, and dig deep to learn all you can about yourself.

If you need some help with questions, there are some great books for resources out there: *If* by Evelyn McFarlane and James

Saywell (there are three versions, with the third version being about romance) and *The Book of Questions* by Gregory Stock, Ph.D.

Besides playing the "Would You Rather" game and asking the hard questions, just simply ask questions. I'm a huge question asker. Some of my friends say I'm an interrogator, because I ask question after question after question. I want to know it all. If you don't ask, you will never know. It's a way to learn and grow. When you stop asking questions, you also stop learning and growing. Whether it's about yourself, someone else, or a place, you never want the questions to stop.

> # The more creative you are with questions, the more you learn about yourself.

What lies behind us and what lies
before us are tiny matters compared
to what lies **within** us.

—Ralph Waldo Emerson

CHAPTER 7: At Your Dinner Table

When you want to know a lot about a person or yourself, ask, "If you could have any five people at your dinner table, living or dead, who would they be and why?" This question allows the respondent to delve inside herself to find out who or what really matters to them.

Think about how people answer this question, especially if the answers are all entertainers or pro ball players. It can give a lot of insight as to their interests and beliefs.

You can use this question with dates, possible dates (like online dating), co-workers, or friends. First make sure you ask yourself the question. Not only because you need to have an answer of your own if you are asking someone else the question, but also because that person may ask you who your five people are. You don't want to say, "I don't know. I haven't given it much thought," when you are expecting them to give you a ready answer.

Don't just say the first five people who come to mind. If you don't know whom you would want, think of people who have influenced your life, or someone you've always wanted to meet. Maybe you think if you could have met him, he would have said something so profound to you that it would have changed your life. Or you might want to dine with someone because she demonstrated strength, willpower, and empowerment at a time in history when women had no rights.

I don't know your reasons for the five people you would choose, but you should. Those people are somewhat representative of who you are. What do they say about you, your personality, or your tastes and interests? Don't choose someone just because he or she might be the popular choice. You could choose someone who is the local hero down your street, or an entrepreneur who was once homeless. You decide who is going to be at your table, and don't let anyone talk you out of your decisions because, after all, they aren't invited to the meal.

What does your choice in dinner table guests say about you?

You are unrepeatable.
There is a magic
about you
that is all
your own…

—D.M. Dellinger

CHAPTER 8: Bring Out Your Leader

People often think of leaders as outgoing, outspoken, or extroverted, when, in fact, those qualities don't define a leader. Whether you are loud or shy, there is a leader in you, and in all of us.

Would you rather be home alone reading rather than speaking before a group of people? Are you more comfortable being a wallflower than the life of the party? Is just about anything more appealing to you than leading a rally? That's okay, because you don't have to be vivacious to lead. You just have to find out your strengths and use them to your advantage.

Lori recently moved to a new city where she didn't know anyone. She was nervous and insecure about meeting new people, but she craved friends. She started a group on meetup.com for women to get together and have fun. If you're not familiar with meetup.com, it's a social site where people go to find others with similar interests. Whether you're looking for adventure, sports, girlfriends, other singles, writing groups, entrepreneurs, or something else, there is a meetup near you. If you don't find what you're looking for, you can start your own. Don't worry—there will be plenty of people joining yours in no time. Lori has over a hundred people on her meetup site, and new people join all the time.

Being in charge of the meetup has allowed Lori to gain self-confidence. People rely on her for scheduling and planning events. Then when they get to the location, they find her, ask her questions, or depend on her for news about the group. Even when they need ideas for a gathering of their own, they ask Lori for advice. Being in charge of the group has allowed Lori to steer away from being shy, because she has to be friendly and inviting to introduce herself constantly to the new people at each function. The group looks to her for new and fun ways to get together, and she loves doing it.

Andrea, a NICU (Neonatal Intensive Care Unit) nurse, is quiet, reserved, shy, and very intelligent. After several months in her first position as a NICU nurse, Andrea's boss asked her to train a new employee. Andrea is confident in what she does, but she had reservations about teaching someone else her knowledge and offering another person her tips.

Although initially hesitant, Andrea excelled so much that her boss asked her to continue conducting this training with every new employee. It never failed; those employees felt a connection with her and continued asking her for advice, even when they were out of training. Andrea willingly gave it and never considered herself to be leadership material, but in teaching others, her abilities were formed. Andrea never wanted to be a leader or pursued opportunities for that to happen; she just always was one. She never went looking for it; it was waiting for a chance to present itself and shine.

You may not set out to be a leader, but plenty of opportunities arise when you are called to action. Don't run away. Step up to challenge! You'll probably surprise yourself. Follow through, because that will allow the leader within you to reveal herself. You may not have a desire to lead a nation or a company, and that's perfectly okay. But there is a leader in you...so let her shine! You may just discover how much you love leading others!

You don't have to set out to be a leader, but when it happens, be ready to shine!

Life
begins
at
the
end
of
your
comfort
zone.

—Neale Donald Walsch

CHAPTER 9: *Keep Challenging Yourself*

People go through the motions in life. Have you ever thought, "Did I unplug the curling iron?" or "Did I turn the oven off?" You become so blasé about life, you stop caring. You get up, go to work, come home, fix the same thing for dinner that you always cook on whatever night it is, and watch television. You stop living life. You forget what it's like to actually live…to do what you want to do, not what your kids, spouse, boss, co-workers, or others want you to do, but what *you* want to do.

When you don't care, you give up on yourself, your future, your goals, and sometimes even life itself. You become a zombie, not remembering what you did yesterday or even this morning, because every day is pretty much the exact day as the day before.

Get out of that mindset and start thinking actively. Challenge yourself. I know the thought of a challenge can be intimidating, but it's nothing you can't overcome. You can do anything you set your heart and mind to do.

Amber had been in customer service for twenty-two years and worked as a hairdresser part-time for almost fifteen years. She knew she wanted to do something else, but she didn't know what. She felt her options were limited. When she had attended college several years ago, she had loved her accounting classes, but she never finished her degree. She knew she couldn't get a job in that field without a degree.

Now in her late thirties, she couldn't allow any more time to go by without doing something about her life. She was up for the challenge, no matter how difficult it might be. She hadn't been in school in twenty years, things would be different this time around. The other students would be much younger than she was, and maybe even more energetic. It might take her longer to do her calculus homework because she needed to refresh her memory of algebra first. But no student would be more motivated, dedicated, or want that degree more than Amber.

Amber knew her limitations; all she could do was all she could do. She couldn't be younger, smarter, or anyone but herself. Classes could prove to be harder for her. She would have to balance school, work, and her family. She also knew without a doubt that no challenge would be too big as long as she took it one day at a time.

That is exactly what she has done. She has proved to herself that no matter how overwhelming something may seem, she is able to not only do it, but to succeed at it as long as she takes it step by step.

Her new norm is different, but she has learned to adjust. She is a better student the second time around because she is more focused and driven. She knows her life is brighter than ever before, all because she chose to challenge herself to have a better future and life.

Strive to challenge yourself weekly or daily. Find ways to challenge yourself. Use your imagination. Stretch yourself. Become the Challenge Expert! Once you start, getting out of your rut will be easier than you ever imagined.

Here is a sampling of some ways you can challenge your mind, body, heart, and soul:

Mind

Puzzles (jigsaw, crossword, Sudoku)
Take a class
Learn a new philosophy, language, or culture
Games (Scrabble, Trivial Pursuit, Taboo, and card games)
Play Devil's Advocate in a conversation
Do 5th Grade Science, Math, or Social Studies. (You may think it will be easy, but you'll likely have to refresh your memory.) Then move on to 6th, 7th and 8th grade lessons.

Read books and/or magazines that might not be your first choice)
Learn the states capitals and each country capitals

Body
Rock climbing
Kayaking
Running
Volleyball
Jump rope
Eat less junk food
Eat a salad three times a week
Eat or drink something that you usually dismiss by saying, "I don't like it."

Heart
Send a card (QuotableCards.com is great).
Say "I'm sorry" or "I love you."
Give an unexpected hug.
Tell someone, "Thank you for being you."
Help someone whose car has stalled on the side of the road.
Become more vulnerable.
Share your story with someone else.
Start a blog about your daily life (you can see mine at jessicarector. com/live-your-greatest-life-blog).

Soul
Skydive
Parasail
Overcome an obstacle
Teach
Learn something new about you
Discover yourself, what you believe, what you value
Stand up for yourself or someone else
Fight for something or someone

There are lots of other ways to challenge yourself. Here are a few more, but I'm sure you can think of a lot on your own. So, go for it. Challenge, challenge, challenge! See what you're made of.

CHALLENGE YOUR...

Creativity:
Write a poem, book or screenplay
Learn how to cross stitch or crochet
Do impersonations
Wear different makeup colors or another fashion style

Business Sense:
Network more often or with different groups
Start a company
Learn another aspect of a company
Find a mentor, or be a mentor to someone who could benefit from your expertise

Yourself:
Exceed your goals and then make them higher
Lifestyle (drink less, go out more, find your dream job, go to another country, go to a concert or play)
Finances (save more, spend less, pay off credit card debt, don't buy new things that you don't really need)
Social life (meet new friends, spend more time with your significant other or find one, have a game night, join meetup.com)

Challenge yourself in more than one area of life at the same time by traveling or volunteering. You will learn about other people, cultures, and customs, and no matter how much you already know about yourself, you will learn even more when you travel. Whether this means becoming more patient while waiting for a delayed flight or learning how to manage your time more effectively by figuring out beforehand that tourist spots close at 3:00 p.m., you will discover something new about yourself whenever you travel away from home and out of your comfort zone. When you travel with someone else, you will appreciate that person more by sharing new experiences with her or him.

Volunteering brings light into your heart and soul and a renewed compassion for humanity, simply because you are stepping outside of yourself to help others. Volunteer at a Red Cross soup kitchen for Thanksgiving and experience the impact you make by serving others. Donate your blood so that someone else might have the chance to live. Give of your time to the student who is struggling at home or in school. A little act of kindness can make all the difference. Volunteer your time, money, or talents. Just get out there and help others.

Stop sleepwalking through your life. Break out of mundane ruts and routines. You need to ignite that spark in your life, and it's easy to do. Do you want a different life? Challenges are your answer! They don't have to be extravagant. You need them in order to remain fully present in life. Set challenging goals for yourself. Don't just say you're going to do them. Write them down on a piece of paper and post it on your refrigerator, vision board, or calendar. Stick to them and follow through until you've reached the goal and met the challenge. Then start some more. Stretch your mind, heart, and body. Stretch your love. Stretch your work ethic. Stretch your dreams, goals, abilities, and skills. Stretch your potential. Stretch your will. Stretch your desires. Stretch, stretch, and stretch some more. *Challenge yourself* to live a better life by making challenges part of your daily or weekly life. You'll soon see the difference in a happier, more present and productive you.

Write daily or weekly challenges as part of your schedule.

MOST OBSTACLES MELT AWAY WHEN WE MAKE UP OUR MINDS TO WALK BOLDLY THROUGH THEM.

—ORISON SWETT MARDEN

CHAPTER 10: How Do You Adapt?

You have probably heard the saying, "The only thing constant in life is change." How do you adapt to change?

Change happens all the time. No matter what you are currently doing in your life, things are bound to change. Your kids grow up, your finances increase or decrease, relationships alter, or someone enters or exits your life. It can't be stopped because life is people, and people change.

Think about the number of people who divorce, even though they were happily married for a number of years. This is because people change a little every day. Maybe we don't see it initially because it's a slow progression. Over time, however, the change becomes more apparent, which results in our acceptance and support of it or our denial and refusal.

You will experience many changes in the process of living your greatest life. You may have doubts and insecurities, and you'll need to work through those. You may wonder who you are, what you really want out of life, or where you see your future unfolding. Make sure you surround yourself with positive, encouraging people who will help you through the journey.

When Sandy decided to study in another country for college, she only thought how interesting it might be. She didn't realize until she arrived that things would be a lot more challenging for her. Although most people spoke English, nothing was familiar to her. She didn't know her way around, and she didn't recognize anything, either—not the brands of food or even herself. Instead of being outgoing and social, she sat in her room feeling alone and sad missing her family and friends.

She would go to class and then come straight home. When she wasn't in her room, she was eating by herself in the kitchen. This was not what she had envisioned when she decided to study overseas. She had thought seeing another country would be exciting, not lonely.

After a couple of weeks of following this same routine, going from her room to class then back to her room again, she decided she wanted more from this experience. It was as though she was fighting against what was right in front of her; she wanted to stop resisting and just embrace it.

She decided she didn't want to be lonely for the next several months. She made up her mind to make friends with the other international students. So she went to the kitchen and sat alongside her roommate at the table. She began a conversation with this girl, whose native language wasn't English. Within a few minutes, they discovered commonalities. They realized they were both missing home, and that being in another country wasn't as easy as either of them had thought it would be. They bonded over their similarities and differences.

The two of them became good friends, and soon they did everything together. They planned a brunch with all the international students, and the group became one. They would eat meals at each other's apartments, go out together, and travel to other countries.

Once Sandy started talking with others in the group, she realized they were dealing with similar emotions. It just took her being open to the opportunities around her and getting out of her comfort zone to enjoy them. Instead of sitting in her room, she decided she was going to adapt to her environment, and her life changed. Sandy explored interesting places, found new friends, and formed lasting bonds.

The more adaptable to change you are, the easier it will be. Don't allow change to control you. Make a conscious effort to be open to experiences that present themselves. You will learn, grow, and become more of the real you.

We are more resilient than we give ourselves credit for. When faced with new situations, we can either make the change easy or hard for ourselves. I choose to make changes as easy as possible because I know that change is inevitable, and the quicker I accept it, the faster I can move on to other things.

You don't have to go to another country to test how well you adapt to change. Think about all the changes that come up in daily life alone.

Carol used the same coffee mug at the office for five years. One day, she couldn't find the mug and refused to use another one. She said, "It just isn't the same." She went out and got coffee instead of using a different mug. Is that you or someone you know?

If you drive to work or take your kids to school the same way every day, and one day you discover that the road is blocked, how do you react? What happens when you run into traffic on your way somewhere? Do you get mad or just take it in stride? Do you allow it to ruin your day, simply because now you are going to be ten minutes late?

The faster you learn to adapt to change, the easier your life will be. People often look at change as a bad thing. They fight tooth and nail against it, especially when they don't like the change that is about to take place. But think about some of the biggest changes in life, and how most of us react to them: getting your first driver's license, going to college, buying a new car, falling in love, getting married, having a baby, buying your first home. These are all major life changes, but we don't struggle with them because they are all things we want. When we don't initiate the change or don't like what we think the result will be, we fight against it. Stop struggling with change. Alter your mindset. Go with it. Embrace it. After all, you can't change it, so you might as well welcome it. That change could be the best thing that ever happens to you.

Adapt to change. The change can be a good thing.

Look under your feet.
The great opportunity
is where you are.
Every place is
under the stars.
Every place is the
center of the universe.

—John Burroughs

CHAPTER 11: *When Change Is Forced Upon You*

Many times, change is forced upon us. We don't want things to change, but someone else decides it's necessary.

Maybe you've worked at the same job for twenty years, and suddenly your boss decides procedures need to change. More common in today's economy, he realizes he can hire someone to replace you who is half your age and thus half the wage. Or maybe the company downsizes and you are the first to go. Has this happened to you or someone you know? How do you deal with it? What do you say or do? It's difficult to accept change when it affects your whole life and your family. How do you *not* take this personally? Isn't it personal? It sure feels like it is.

Mike suffered a great loss. His partner of ten years had died unexpectedly. He was walking through life in a daze, barely able to put one foot in front of the other. His finances became such a shambles that he filed for bankruptcy just to get some relief. He was depressed and couldn't envision a positive future for himself. He could barely manage getting through each day.

As the days turned into months, his depression diminished, but he still had no hope or vision for his future. He didn't feel as defeated or low, but he knew he still had a long way to go. Putting himself out in the world to meet and interact with others was the last thing on his mind.

Almost a year after his partner died, he walked into the gym to do his daily workout routine and went over to the exercise machine he always used, when he glanced up and saw someone looking at him from across the room. When their eyes met, they instantly knew it was magical. They briefly spoke before leaving the gym and decided to meet for dinner that night. They moved in together two weeks later and have been together ever since.

Mike didn't go to the gym that day looking for his future partner. He didn't think his mind or his heart were ready to find someone else yet, but this person was exactly who he needed. Mike and his partner complement each other. Their love for one another can be seen from across the room, just like how it was when their eyes met for the first time.

Mike could have easily allowed his negative mindset to overtake his life, but he knew he couldn't continue to live that way. After suffering so much loss, depression, and financial ruin, he'd had no hope for the future. It took time, but with each day, his attitude changed just a little, allowing his mind and heart to be open to the opportunities that awaited him. Then, when the time was right, the universe gave him exactly what and who he needed.

Mike now lives a life of abundance filled with love, financial stability, and emotional happiness. He never imagined his future could be this bright.

When change is forced upon us, it is never easy. Do you spring into action and say, "What now?" and go searching for a new opportunity? Instead of allowing yourself to sink into depression or wallow in self-pity, think of what you have yet to do in life. Think of an adventure you can go on—then plan it and go! You will meet other people and open new doors of opportunity that never could've been found while staying cooped up inside alone.

When change is forced upon you, how do you respond? Do you wallow in self-pity? Do you spend several days lying on the couch depressed, not knowing what will come your way while hoping someone will knock on your door and say, "You are just the person I've been looking for?"

Have you lost a job, found another one, and ended up liking the second one better, or you made more money doing the same amount of work? When Jamie was eight months pregnant with her third child, she discovered her husband was cheating on her. She confronted him about it, and he admitted it. They soon split, and she was left heartbroken to raise three children without a spouse. She moved in with her sister and brother-in-law, who had two kids of their own, which was difficult. She never envisioned her life this way.

Even though they lived several states away from each other, Jamie talked every year on her birthday with Chad, a guy she dated about twelve years earlier. Chad was a few years younger than Jamie and had other priorities, so it hadn't worked out when they dated previously. The year Jamie and her husband split, Chad didn't call her for her birthday, so she called him to find out why. Jamie and Chad ended up talking for hours. They met a month later for the weekend, and then started a long distance relationship.

Jamie doesn't want anyone to endure the pain of a cheating spouse, but she was glad things worked out the way they did in her life, because she and Chad married a few years later. She is happier with him than she ever was with her first husband. It didn't take her long to realize that all the pain and heartbreak of her initial situation was a blessing in disguise. If not for it, then she would have never married Chad, the one she had wanted to marry the first time they dated many years ago.

Sometimes you have to go through the hurt in order to live the life you are meant to live. You can't allow that suffering to keep you down. You have to forge through to the other side because you don't know what or who might be waiting there. The heartbreak is only temporary. In time, it will pass. While you process the incident, think of Jamie and her tenacity to move forward. Yes, she felt the pain and hurt that came with the loss and the major change she had never expected, but she didn't let that keep her down. She didn't allow that to hold her back and keep her from pursuing what she wanted in life. She still looked at the future with possibilities and knew that love was out there for her. She seized the moment when she took advantage of an opportunity that presented itself to rekindle her love with Chad.

When change is thrust upon us, it is really an opportunity in disguise. You can find your passion, start your own business, or find love. It's your time to discover what you desire. Do you want to go back to school, begin a networking group, or teach dance?

We all need time to process, but change is not a bad thing. Don't spend the time lounging around wishing things were different. If you let a few days go by, then a week will fly. Before you know it, a month has passed and you still haven't seized the opportunity. Don't view change as a death sentence or the end of the world. This is the time to make things happen that you've always wanted—to do all those things you've put off for so long. Don't wait any longer!

This change could be the best thing that has happened to you. You weren't willing to make the decision for yourself, so someone else made it for you. Now, embrace the change. Think of it as a gift. Take advantage of it and go out there to discover, find, explore. Imagine what you can achieve and accomplish. Think of your new world, and realize that you are one step closer to living your greatest life. Go out there and make it happen. Go out there and seize the opportunity for a better life. Now is your time!

When change is forced upon you, seize the opportunity.

Find life experiences
and **swallow** them
whole. **Travel.**
Meet many people.
Go down some
dead ends and
explore dark alleys.
Try everything.
Exhaust yourself
in the glorious
pursuit of life.

—Lawrence K. Fish

CHAPTER 12: *Traveling*

We are all a work in progress. No matter how much we know about ourselves there is always more to learn, because we are constantly changing with every new life experience.

I feel like I know a lot about myself, but every time I'm fortunate enough to travel I always learn something else about myself. It doesn't have to be anything earth shattering, but I always discover at least one thing that I didn't really know or understand.

I worked at a major airline about fourteen years ago. I needed a job and randomly applied there thinking I might work my way up the ladder. At twenty-three years of age, I took my first international trip to London, Paris, and Dundalk (a city outside of Dublin). This trip was all it took to get bitten by the travel bug.

Each time I go somewhere, I'm always interested to learn what I will discover about myself. I took a trip to Scotland and Wales with my mom, and when we were making our return journey home, we had to first board a train, which would take us to the airport. I walked quite a ways in front of my mom and kept rushing her, certain that we would miss the train. I kept turning around to make sure she was behind me, but I rushed on ahead, determined not to miss the train. The next one wouldn't come for another thirty minutes, and that would cut it too close for us to catch our flight. I thought if I could get to the train before it took off, I could hold it until my mom got there.

I made it to the train in time, as did my mom. We even had a few minutes to spare. As the train took off, I realized we were on the wrong train, but it was too late. We were stuck there. My complete lack of patience had been a fruitless effort.

We got off the train then had to board it once again to take it back to where we had started. We then waited to catch the right train. If I had taken two extra minutes to figure things out correctly the first time, we never would have been in that situation. Because of this unnecessary delay, we literally had to run through the airport to get to our flight, which we ended up catching. I added so much extra stress to our trip by being impatient, when I didn't need to be. If I could have just breathed a little and relaxed a bit, that whole process would have been much smoother.

When was the last time you were impatient when you didn't need to be? When did you create unnecessary stress on yourself or someone else?

I learned a great lesson on my first trip to North Carolina with my boyfriend at the time. I took a rolling suitcase and a garment bag for our weekend trip. He brought a duffel bag. He even told me before we left, "Whatever luggage you take, you will have to carry." I thought nothing of it; after all, how hard could it be to pull a rolling suitcase with one hand while carrying a garment bag in the other?

Little did I know that I would be taking what seemed like a long distance hike in high heels through the airport to get to our gate. After a few gates, he knew I needed help carrying my garment bag because I also had my carry-on bag slung over my shoulder. Oh, did I forget to mention that?! This was before the strict (and unreasonable) carry-on luggage requirements were in place that we have now. So, I was allowed to carry all of these items with me into the airplane cabin. Yes, I technically had three pieces of luggage for a weekend, but I didn't know what I would want to wear. Or, should I say, I didn't know what I would be in the mood to wear.

I learned from that one trip not to take more than what I'm going to use; well, I learned...somewhat. When I go on trips, I still don't know what I'm going to want to wear. But I have to be realistic. If I'm going for three days, I'm probably not going to wear five different pairs of shoes. I could go with three.

I know that I can bring a selection of things, but I just need to make sure that all the items can be worn with everything else I'm bringing. This all makes sense in theory, but no matter how well I think I'm packing, I always come home with items I never wore on the trip and wonder, *Why did I pack so much?*

To experience the rejuvenation that travel brings, you don't have to travel abroad; you can go to a local bed and breakfast or simply go visit your parents out of town. Where did you go on your last trip and with whom? What did you learn about yourself? You may like to explore new things and visit exciting places for the thrill and adventure of it, but take that opportunity to learn something new about yourself as well. It will help you get to know yourself even better.

> Travel as often as possible. It will give you the opportunity to learn more about yourself.

BELIEVE WITH ALL OF YOUR
HEART
THAT YOU WILL DO
WHAT YOU WERE
MADE
TO DO.

—ORISON SWETT MARDEN

STEP 2: EXPLORING WHAT YOU WANT

At first thought, exploring what you want may seem easy to do. After all, we all want something—a bigger house, more money, better behaved kids, a new car, a flat screen TV, a media room, your spouse to remember your anniversary without your having to remind him, a career you love, more time, better relationships, or even five minutes of quiet time. We always want something.

Your task is not to figure out how many more material things you can acquire, but what it is *you* really want? What does your heart say? What is the one thing that is truly missing from your life? How can you get it?

CHAPTER 13: *What Do You Really Want?*

It's funny how we can list a million material things that we want, but sometimes it is difficult to figure out what we really want in the larger scope of our lives. You want a better life, but what does that mean? You want to lose weight, but what does that mean? It's the weight, but it's not the weight. It is what's beneath the weight. It's what's holding you back. You want a career you love, but you never take the time to search for one. Why? Do you think you aren't qualified, so you don't apply because you're certain you won't get hired anyway? Maybe you want to find love or just make friends with people, but you rarely leave the house. Are you scared you'll get rejected? Do you think you aren't "good enough?"

What is it you really want? What's keeping you from having it? Be honest with yourself. We all want something in our lives. What is it *you* want?

Carlene has a gift for bringing people together. Her aura is seen from across the room, but that is not how it has always been. Carlene shares her amazing outlook on life:

"Challenges and changes are the staples of my diet that allow the seeds of opportunity to grow. I view them as a gift of purpose, and with great anticipation, I am shown that purpose over time. I am a very passionate woman. Passion is the energy of emotion that turns my dreams into reality. It allows me to envision change and to draw near the tools needed for that change and the power to make a difference.

"The heaviest of loads created the landscape of my life. It provided trenches, peaks and valleys, but it gave my life depth and opportunity as well. The rocks that were cast at me came in the forms of childhood poverty, physical, sexual, and mental abuse, and then later, through a physically and mentally abusive marriage. I learned to use these rocks as stepping-stones. I refused to let the lack of a college education derail my success.

"Life became my daily lesson. I was once asked, 'Is it hard to be this positive all the time?' My answer—and I mean this with ALL of my heart— was that life was **much** harder the other way around, meaning, when I was consumed by negativity. Staying positive has been the easiest thing I have ever done. I decided that I would no longer force someone to be happy or successful at my own expense. I accepted the differences and walked away from the imbalance. The more I removed the negative, the faster success came. I was given the strength to remove negative relationships from my life, and the best part was that I learned to believe in me. I was no longer driven by the approval of others; instead, I now sought approval from myself. I accepted everything about me and made no apologies for it!

"By age forty, I had reached my goal to earn a six-figure income. By forty-one, I had become the CEO of my own company. Within its first year, it was valued at one million dollars. I have started two 501-c3 charitable organizations and currently serve as the vice president of another. I have also had the honor of being named Ambassador of the Year for four different cities, and I continue to serve on countless boards for various groups."

"Accept yourself, accept others, and stay focused. Fuel your faith and not your fears. Focus on what you want in life and talk about only those things, not about what you don't want. It will take practice, but better yet, it will work. Understand that who you are and what you have experienced is not a mistake. Stop trying to improve areas you are weak in; focus on your strengths and surround yourself with a team of people who are strong in your areas of weakness.

"Live your life in a blaze of glory; you have earned your flame. Allow your passion to burn bright. Be that flame that ignites change; light up the world and inspire. Burn a path for others to follow and allow it to remind you of where you have been. Light up the darkness, bring comfort to the hurting, and view what's ahead. Life is giving you a grand and majestic view, so shine on!"

Things don't happen overnight. All of Carlene's experiences molded her positive attitude and perspective and led her to the life she leads now. The painful journey of her early years motivated her to create a better future. She chose to stop allowing people or situations to dictate her life or mindset. She took control of her life, and that has made all the difference in her outlook and her success.

It takes time for people to be aligned so they are ready to step into one another's lives. Whether it's a future mate, boss, client, or friend, that person needs to be prepared for you, mentally, physically, spiritually, and emotionally. If you meet him one second before you are meant to, he won't be ready to receive you. Maybe you're ready for him now, but he isn't ready for you because he still has some growing to do. You might think you have all you need to meet that person, but maybe you need to learn another lesson, become more open, or finish something that lingers in your life undone. You might need one more experience to prepare you for the career, life partner, passion, calling, or love that's perfect for you—in other words, to prepare you for the life you want and that you were meant to live. Be open to everything.

What do you really want? What does your heart say? Listen closely to it. It may be speaking to you, but you're not really listening to it. Be open to the opportunities that present themselves. You don't want to miss something that is right in front of you and just what you've been waiting for, though you may not recognize it at first. Maybe you've never really known what you want, or you've pushed the thought aside thinking it will never happen. Now it's right here, right now, waiting for you. Reach out and take it! Or, search for it proactively and make it happen. You have all that you need to get exactly what you want. This life is yours for the taking. Go grab it!

Live with no regrets. Don't ever say, "Gosh, I wonder what would have happened if..." You can *know* what would have happened, because you *did* it. Yes, you may get hurt in the process. Yes, you may not like it. But you will never wonder, *What if...?* That's satisfying enough to make up for getting hurt or not liking the choice you made. You can recover from those. But if you don't do something, the chance will pass, and then it will be gone.

You know where you are now. You can always come back to that place...but that chance—that opportunity—won't always be there. Step forward, slide down, or jump off. Just do it! And never look back.

> # Proactively pursue what you really want.

You are here to
enable the world
to live more amply,
with greater vision,
and with a finer spirit
of hope and achievement.
You are here to
enrich the world.

—Woodrow Wilson

CHAPTER 14: *Your Vision*

If you don't have a vision board, you need one. If you have one, but it's been at least five years since you made it, make another one. If yours is hiding behind your dresser, under your bed or in your closet, dust it off and hang it up some place where you have to walk by it every day. You must have a vision board!

For those of you unfamiliar with a vision board, let me start by giving you a list of the materials you will need, and then I will explain the concept to you.

TOOLS NEEDED:
Cardboard (any color)
Magazines (variety of them if possible, but not a necessity)
Scissors
Glue or a glue stick (tape will also work)
4 Thumbtacks (or whatever you want to use when you're ready to hang it)

You can make it as simple or creative as you want. I used scrap-booking scissors to cut fancier edges on my photos. I also bought cardboard that is red on one side and bright yellow on the other. I cut it in half and taped the two halves back together, with yellow on the left side and red on the right. This worked out perfectly for me because those two colors just happen to be the two colors that best describe me. On the yellow side, I put my personal life items, and on the red side, I put items representative of my career and professional life.

You can do it any way you want, because it's your vision board. You don't have to put personal and professional things separate. You can combine them in any way you want.

A vision board is for things that you envision in your life. Ask yourself what's in your heart. Discover what you really want and put it on the board. Go through the magazines you have and cut out pictures, sayings, words, faces, letters, and anything else you want on your vision board that will perfectly capture what you want for your life. On my personal side it says, "I want a hot, sexy, smart man." Those are all words I cut out from different articles or ads. None of them match each other, and they are all different shapes, colors, and sizes. Lower on the left side of the board, I have a picture of George Clooney, with "Finally we meet," across his torso. I also have sayings like, "There's never been a better time to focus on YOU," and "Go where others won't," and "I live in the moment."

On my red side, I have pictures of a video camera (for my talk show), a studio, and a computer with the word "blogger" by it. I love sayings, so I put some on this side as well, "Leading out loud means doing something...standing up for something," and, "The JessICAREctor Show" (yes I cut out red letters for the ICARE part too), "Relentlessly pursue," and "Make a difference."

I have several things right down the middle of the board, such as, "Can one voice change the world?" ... "HOPE" ... "Live Your Greatest Life" ... "The Power of 1" ... "Believe" ... "I love life" and "Never give up." I also have a huge picture of Oprah right in the middle of my board. She signifies inspiration and motivation to me.

When I look at the board, I am inspired by a combination of pictures and sayings. I definitely have more inspirational and motivational thoughts, quotes, and quips on my professional side, with more pictures (such as couples holding hands) on my personal side.

My board encompasses a lot of who I am. It is full but not crammed. I love looking at it, because each time I see it, I focus on something I haven't seen in a while. It's new to me every time I look at it.

When you are creating your vision board, what do you believe in your heart of hearts? What do you deeply desire in your soul? What do you dream about? Put it on your board and watch your reality change. Create your board with you in mind—what you want, what your heart desires, what your spirit sings. Make sure it's inspiring and motivating for you, because when you look at this board, it needs to remind you to be proactive—to go out into the world and make your vision a reality.

If you don't envision your wants, desires, and dreams, they will not come to pass. Believe they will happen, and then envision them. That's when they will be your reality. If you don't have the belief as the foundation, how are you going to truly see it fully and clearly? You may envision a portion of it, but you won't get the whole picture. Believe it, envision it, and then it will happen. What does your vision board look like? Did you separate your personal and professional life? Did you put them all together? What's the reason for the way you designed your board? What were you feeling when you were making it? Grab a couple of friends and have a girls' night when you all get together and make them. You can laugh with each other as you flip though the magazines. You will be making memories while creating your future. Who better to do it with than friends or family?

When you finish making this fine piece of art, hang it someplace where you will see it every day and be motivated and inspired to work toward your goal of living your greatest life!

> # Believe! Envision your reality and create your vision today.

WALK WITH THE DREAMERS,
THE BELIEVERS, THE COURAGEOUS,
THE CHEERFUL, THE PLANNERS,
THE DOERS, THE SUCCESSFUL PEOPLE
WITH THEIR HEADS IN THE CLOUDS
AND THEIR FEET ON THE GROUND.
LET THEIR SPIRIT IGNITE A FIRE
WITHIN YOU TO LEAVE THIS WORLD
BETTER THAN WHEN YOU FOUND IT...

—WILFERD PETERSON

CHAPTER 15: Channeling Your Energy

How are you using your energy? What does it say about you? Do you hesitantly get out of bed in the morning or are you eager to face each day?

When you get out of bed, get your energy flowing. Be enthusiastic to face your day. Put a skip in your step, as you look forward to what might happen as the day progresses.

Do you feel under the weather the minute you get to the office? How do you face the day? Are you walking with confidence, with your shoulders back and head held up high? Or are you slouched over, as though you have already been defeated?

When you enter a room, do people think *I need to meet that person...*? Are people automatically drawn to you? What is your aura saying? You probably have an idea of how people respond to you when you walk into a room. If you don't know, ask your friends their opinions. I'm not talking about gaining attention by being obnoxious and loud. When you stand with confidence and self-assurance, people respond accordingly. They want to know more. They want to meet you and get to know you. Walk through life knowing who you are and what you have to offer the world.

If your energy is quiet, you might be overlooked. People won't notice you're coming or going. Change this by altering your perspective on yourself. Know you are attractive, intelligent, witty, vivacious, and giving. It's not arrogance. It's confidence. When you know who you are, others will pick up on it. They will be pulled toward you without even realizing it, because you aren't drawing them to you intentionally.

Dr. Jill Bolte Taylor says, "Please take responsibility for the energy you bring into this space." You are responsible for your energy—the energy you create and bring to others.

You've probably known people who just have a certain aura—a level of positive energy that you sense whenever you're around them. You can be in a crowded gathering, but you know the minute they have arrived. People turn around to look at them and then swarm around them. They are never left alone. It's as though there is something magical about them.

You can be one of those people. It's in the way you present yourself. It's never too late to create it, but it all begins with you. You may ask, "Jessica, that's great. I want to have that aura; how do I create it?"

Look in the mirror with your head held high and your shoulders back. Yes, it may seem like you're pushing your chest out, but it's okay…you'll likely have to push it out slightly. It may feel a little weird or awkward at first. But when you do assume this posture on a regular basis, you will get used to it, and soon it will feel natural.

If you don't have a full-length mirror, get one. Walk toward it. Watch your body language. How do you walk? What does it say about you? If you don't know what it says, ask a friend. How do you dress? That's the first impression people get from you.

After you feel comfortable with the mirror exercise, make sure you are walking that way in your everyday life. You will have to make a conscious effort to do this at first, because it may not come naturally to you. Your posture says a lot about you. If you are slumped over staring at the ground, it comes off as though you are insecure or shy. Stand upright as though you are the greatest thing alive. Be careful, however, to not come across as being full of yourself, because that will turn people off. Don't say you are the greatest thing, but know you are *you*—a wonderful, beautiful, loving person.

The way you stand, walk, and present yourself makes a huge difference in how others perceive you. Work on your handshake. There is nothing worse than meeting someone for the first time, and when she shakes your hand she gives you only her fingers, like she is a queen.

What's a proper handshake? It's one where your hand fits firmly into the other person's hand, and you give it a firm shake. Don't be wimpy. You will be surprised how much a handshake says about you. If your first impression isn't good, you have to work triple hard to undo it. Why not give a great impression from the beginning?

Dress with confidence. Be stylish. If you are asking yourself, "Am I stylish?" Then the answer is most likely, "No, you aren't." That doesn't mean you have to dress like everyone else. What do you want your style to say about you? Dress your age. Don't wear miniskirts if you are not a teenager. If you are in the professional world, don't wear something too risqué. Each person has her own individual style.

Change it up; wear something you might not usually wear. Create your own style but don't be a fashion *faux pas*. Make sure your style fits your personality and what you are trying to portray. If you aren't sure, hire a style coach or ask your friends to tell you what your usual style says about you, meaning the impression it gives, and how they think you need to improve it.

Tim brands himself as a Rocker Life Coach, so he dresses in a style that is typically perceived as the rocker look: jeans, boots, and longer hair. His style fits his persona, and it's perfect. You don't need to have the same style as everyone else. Make sure your style aligns with how you want others to see you.

When your style, handshake, and confidence all line up, others will take note. When you have the self-assurance that you can do anything you set your mind to doing, you will have an unspoken energy—something that you won't be able to put your finger on, and that will cause others to be drawn to you, even if they don't know why. They just know they are. Then when you walk into the room, all eyes will be on you and everyone will be thinking, *I must meet her.*

Jump out of bed. Create your own ENERGY!

If you have
a preference,
voice it.
If you have
a question,
ask it.
If you want
to cry, bawl.
If you need
help, raise
your hand
and jump up
and down!

—Kristin Armstrong

CHAPTER 16: *The Hardest Thing to Do*

Are you able to ask for help when you know you need it? Do you think asking for help is a sign a weakness, as though you can't handle things yourself? And if anything, you know you aren't weak. You are a strong, independent, self-assured woman. You are not weak. Since you don't want to be perceived as weak, the last thing you will do is ask for help. You would rather muddle through and figure it out on your own, even if it means not always having the greatest success. Failing seems better than asking for help because you can rationalize failing, and then you wouldn't necessarily have to tell someone else you had intended to do a certain thing in the first place. You could do it quietly, and then if you failed, you could ignore it ever happened. Whereas, if you asked for help, someone somewhere would know things were not quite right. They would know you were weak, which is the worst thing possible. You just wouldn't have that.

In addition, asking for help means putting yourself out there. It means the possibility of rejection—of someone telling you 'no'. Take the sign of weakness and multiply by the fear of rejection and you have a 'no way in hell will I ask for help' kind of mentality. Are you convinced that people should *know* when you need help and offer it to you?

This mindset will bring you nothing but a lot of misery and heartache. First of all, people cannot read your mind. Secondly, we all know what it's like to be told 'no', and as much as we dread hearing it, it doesn't destroy us. Pinch yourself or even put your right index finger on your left forearm. Do you feel it? You are, in fact, still alive. So when he told you 'no', the worst that could happen, didn't. You are still here. So don't let the possibility of hearing 'no' stand in your way. If you do, you will never try, risk, or accomplish anything. You will be exactly where you are now. And you know that's not where you want to be.

No is a two-letter word that can teach you a lot when you understand that it can't damage you unless you allow it to. Don't let it! Refuse to let a simple two-letter word stand in your way of the job, relationship, finances, or love you want.

While watching a TV commercial sponsored by a non-profit organization whose mission is to help those suffering famine in Africa, Leslie was surprised by her reaction. She had seen many such commercials in the past, but this time she sat on the sofa and wept. She had always thought, *When I have more money, I will do something to help.* After seeing this commercial, she decided the people in Africa couldn't wait for her help, and that's when the idea came to her. Leslie knew it was going to be a challenge, but this was her time to do something about it.

It began just like that, as an idea. She didn't know how she was going to pull it off. Just thinking about all she had to do for the event was a little overwhelming. She didn't know anyone who had raised money for a cause, and she had never done anything like it before. She didn't know where to begin.

Leslie knew she couldn't do it on her own. She told her idea to a few friends who volunteered to help her organize a trivia game night and a silent auction event. It was up to her to find the auction items, trivia questions and prizes, and guests.

Without further hesitation, she just jumped in and started. She was initially scared of rejection when she called a few restaurants and stores asking for donations. She was told *no* more often than *yes*, but that didn't deter her. It motivated her even more. Leslie decided to go to these businesses in person because she thought it would be harder for them to tell her *no* in person. She was nervous as she opened the doors to the first restaurant. She didn't want to hear another *no*. The manager of the place not only told her *yes*, but he donated several things to her. After she received this positive response, every other door became easier to walk through.

All told, about sixty silent auction items were donated, in addition to raffle prizes and the trivia prize. A lot of people volunteered their time to plan and work the event, and more people attended the event than she had expected.

Leslie thinks a lot of people have it in their hearts to give and help others, but they don't know what to do. They just need to be given the opportunity. They won't seek it, but if you ask them, they are more than willing to help.

Leslie raised more than $1,200 for the children in Africa. Imagine what you can do for the causes you believe in.

If you are like Leslie and you hate the thought of rejection, asking for help may not be easy. You may be told *no*, but don't let that stop you from pushing forward. Persevere through it, and you will accomplish more than you dreamed possible.

Positive people in your life know that asking for help is like asking to be rejected, but they will also be the first ones to do what it takes to ensure you follow your own path, have a brighter future, or pursue your dreams. Asking for what you need is not a sign of weakness. It actually shows strength. It demonstrates that you know your limits. What you want to achieve may not be possible without the help of others, and you have the self-confidence to know that putting yourself out there may help you accomplish your goals and dreams.

Consider your life for a few moments. What do you want to accomplish that is beyond the scope of your own abilities, experiences, or finances? How can you ask for help? First, don't be afraid of rejection. Being afraid to ask holds you back from attaining what is important to you. Don't let fear keep you from accomplishing your goals. If you don't ask, you will never know the answer. It may be exactly what you want to hear.

Secondly, be able to express what you need clearly and articulately. Don't expect others to know what you need. Don't say,

"No, that's fine, I can do it by myself," when what you really mean is, "I need you to help me make dinner, clean the house, or fix the washer."

Finally, ask for help more often. The more you do it, the more proficient you will become at asking in a way that invites people to *want* to help you.

Being afraid to ask holds you back from what is really important. We all need help in our lives. We aren't meant to live cut off from everyone else. People like to be needed. Leaning on someone else or relying on a friend to assist you when you need it gives people a reason to be. Don't take them for granted, but also don't hesitate to ask for their help when you need it. Because, trust me, they will soon be asking for yours.

> # Don't fear asking for help; it's a sign of strength.

You gain strength,
courage, and confidence
by every experience
in which you really stop
to look fear in the face...
Do the thing you
think
you cannot do.

—Eleanor Roosevelt

STEP 3: UNCOVERING YOUR FEARS

CHAPTER 17: *Our Commonality*

There is something we all have in common, and that is the fear of something. We often don't realize it, and usually we don't acknowledge it, but we all have fears. Many people think it's a sign of weakness to admit their fears. Others think if they ignore their fears, then they don't exist. Fear of heights, enclosed spaces, and public speaking are common. How do you face your fears?

When I asked Wendy to share her story, she was glad to do so. As you'll see from what she went through, she had no choice but to face her fears.

Wendy began by explaining, "Sadly, it has been generally accepted in divorce culture that parents act with hostility and negativity towards each other. It is partly due to such acceptance that parental alienation is the only form of child abuse that has not received a great deal of public attention or outrage. To put it simply, parental alienation is when one parent uses behaviors and actions to damage or destroy a child's relationship with the other parent. These can range from mild and subtle to extreme and blatant. Regardless of the severity of the tactics used, parental alienation is child abuse and causes lifelong damage to the child."

Wendy continued, "As is very common, I had never heard the term 'parental alienation' before, and I was completely unaware that my children and I were being victimized by my ex-husband as a result of these tactics. My relationships with all three of my children had been nothing but extremely close and positive in every way. All I knew was that one of my children was suddenly and unexplainably scathing and hostile towards me to the point of refusing to communicate with me or see me at all. For many months, I lived in total agony, confusion, disbelief, and fear over the transformation I witnessed in my child, not realizing that he was being mentally abused by his father.

"When a friend of mine told me about parental alienation, I was astonished to learn that I was not alone. It also made me spring into immediate action to take whatever steps were necessary to save my child from an abusive situation.

"Since the father of my child had been refusing to send our child to visit me for nearly a year, and therefore was in violation of custody orders, my first step was to get legal assistance and intervention. Being completely naïve and unknowledgeable about the family court system, I believed that the judge would help my child since the abusive situation was completely documented and indisputable, even by my ex-husband's own admission. Little did I know that I would put into motion what is now known as 'the most corrupt family court case in the history of Tarrant County, Texas.'

"There were more obstacles within the situation that I had to overcome. How does one endure death threats and losing every penny she has while fighting to save the life of her child from an abusive situation that is unrecognized by many people, including therapists, and that is actually frequently rewarded and assisted by our family court system? At times I felt truly hopeless, and it seemed impossible for me to overcome the many obstacles that were larger than anything I had ever imagined. It was the love I have for my children that gave me the energy, inspiration, and motivation I needed to persevere. I had to exhaust every possibility of attempting to save my child from an abusive situation. When facing obstacles, always remember what your ultimate goal is, and ask yourself, 'What is the worst thing that can happen if I continue to face this obstacle?' Then ask yourself, 'What is the worst that can happen if I **don't** continue to fight this obstacle?'

"The sad reality is alienating parents almost never discontinue alienating behaviors in attempts to damage or destroy their children's relationships with the other parent, even when the children reach adulthood. However, this obstacle can be transformed into an opportunity. That is the path I have chosen. Through parental alienation awareness and education efforts around the world, I am able to help others, which has been personally healing and empowering. My two teenagers are doing remarkably well. I have proven to them they will always receive unconditional love and acceptance from me, regardless of any outside pressures or influences. Through the trials and ultimately triumph of this situation, I have seen them grow into compassionate and caring young people. I couldn't be more proud of them for their strength and wisdom, which was surely gained through this experience. My oldest daughter remains alienated from me, however. I remain hopeful and optimistic, with continued reminders of my unwavering love and acceptance of her, that we will be close again soon."

Certain opportunities will arise in our lives that allow us to uncover, confront, and conquer our fears. Are you going to let that chance pass you by, or are you going to grab it by the horns and take control?

Be open to opportunities to uncover, confront, and conquer your fears.

I will not tiptoe
through life
only to arrive
at death safely.

–Anonymous

CHAPTER 18: How Fear Can Help You

What are you afraid of? Heights, enclosed spaces, spiders? Public Speaking, failure, depression? Everyone can identify with being scared of something. What scares you?

Recognizing your fear can catapult you to new, undiscovered heights. Meredith's story shows how acknowledging and confronting her fears allowed her to free herself and help others.

Meredith begins her story by saying, "Much of my life was spent trying to fit a mold that I now realize does not exist. I allowed circumstances and people to influence me to such a degree that I felt helpless and out of control. My only way of coping was to control my eating; in other words, my life was subsumed by the ineffective behaviors of an eating disorder. I continued to use those behaviors for eighteen years. I never wanted to give them up and thought it would be useless to try, anyway. Whenever I was confronted about my eating disorder, I would yell at whoever was trying to help me because I refused to believe that I could get well. I thought I was the one exception to recovery—that it was simply not possible for me.

"It was not until I entered a graduate program in counseling in 2010 that I began to view my life in terms of choice. I had to stop pretending that I had no control and instead needed to take charge of my behaviors. I knew that in order to help clients in the future, I had to be well myself. I could not be consumed with an eating disorder and effectively help anyone who would come to me for counseling. I decided it was time to give up what I had clung to for more than half of my life. I called my former therapist and told her I was ready to resolve my issues for good, and I headed back into weekly sessions where I finally started to do the work it takes to let go.

"I will not pretend that it was easy or quick, as I had already been to residential treatment twice and had worked with at least three outpatient therapists. I waivered for some time, fighting myself and fighting God over why I deserved anything, let alone recovery. Slowly, hope began to show itself to me a piece at a time. It had actually been there all along, buried inside of me, but hope could not be a part of my life until I was willing to be open and to choose to have it each moment of each day.

"Today, I am in recovery and learning what it truly means to love myself. I am also able to maintain clients in a private counseling practice, continue writing my award-winning mental health blog, and sustain a wonderful relationship with my fiancé. Whenever I can, I take advantage of opportunities to share my story because I believe that each time I share where I have been, my past loses more control over me."

Confronting your fears will help you achieve the greatness you desire in your life. Hold yourself accountable for your fear. It's your responsibility to take action to dissolve your fear. The longer you allow it to exist, the more control you allow it to have over you. Take back your power and realize that you can achieve success in your life, just as Meredith has done.

You may be thinking, *Jessica, being scared to ask for help is not the same as* _____ (the fear you have). But it is. The actual fear isn't relevant. What matters is that, despite what the fear is, it's crippling you. It's stopping you from achieving, accomplishing, and moving forward. It's keeping you in the same place you've always been...the place you don't want to be. All fears start small, but over time they grow and expand. They end up so large in our heads that we can't wrap our minds around overcoming them. We don't know how to move past them. That's what fears do—they stop you, they control you, and they exert power over you. Face your fears today and take back your power.

> # No matter the exact fear, you allow it to cripple you.

Twenty years from now you will be more disappointed by the things you didn't do than by the ones you did. So throw off the bowlines. Sail away from the safe harbor. Catch the trade winds in your sails. **Explore. Dream. Discover.**

—Unknown

CHAPTER 19: *Recognize Your Fears*

What will it take to confront your fears? Why do you allow someone else to have power over you? Do you enjoy something controlling you?

I don't know about you, but I don't want anyone or anything to have power or control over me. I control me, just as you should control you. So what's stopping you from taking back your power?

The first step is to recognize your fear. Then admit to yourself the power it has over you. Be specific.

It stops me from doing _____.
I don't like how I feel when_____.
It keeps me from _____.
I don't feel comfortable _____.

Where do you want to go? What do you want to be doing, feeling, and accomplishing?

I would like to _____.
I want to feel _____.
I want to have more _____.
I'm looking for _____.
I want to be able to _____.

All the places you want to go and all the things you want to do, feel, and accomplish are attainable. They are within your grasp.

You just have to reach out your hand for them. They are right there in front of you. You can do it. Just stretch forward. Make it your reality. It's not just about thinking you can overcome your fears; you need to believe and know you can. I believe and know you can!

What will it take for you to do it? Do you need to lose your job, house, or loved one? Do you need to hit bottom? Do you want to continue sleepwalking through life?

Nothing about it is easy, but as the saying goes, "Nothing worth having comes easily." If I can do it, so can you. I've heard that 99.9% of the time what we fear never happens. We build it up to be something it's not. It starts out small, and we allow it to grow, expand, and progress over time. We give it permission to be something it isn't. That sentence is key: WE GIVE IT PERMISSION TO BE SOMETHING IT ISN'T. You can choose not to give it permission by taking the power away from it. Instead of thinking, *What bad thing will happen if I confront*_____ (your fear)? Think, *What GOOD thing will happen when I confront*_____ (your fear)? When you alter your mindset, the outcome will also change.

> # Stop giving fear permission to control your life.

What would you attempt to do if you knew you would not fail?

—Unknown

CHAPTER 20: *Confront Your Fears*

Make a goal to not fear the fear. You want to control the fear. When you are scared of the fear and what might happen if you confront it, you hide. You take cover and never come out, hoping and even expecting it to disappear. It won't! Take a step each day toward conquering your fear. These don't need to be large steps, just small ones. Construct a plan and don't forget to follow through.

Part of life is failure. Zig Ziglar once said, "Failure is an event not a person." We all heard of stories where people have "failed" or not got what they wanted when they wanted.

You may have heard the story of how J. K. Rowling, the author of the Harry Potter series, was rejected by twelve publishers when she sent them her manuscript for book one in the series. I bet they are kicking themselves now. Dr. Seuss' first book manuscript was rejected by twenty-seven publishers. Elvis Presley was fired after his first performance in the Grand Ole Opry. Bill Gates dropped out of Harvard and started his first business, which failed. Walt Disney was fired by a newspaper for "lack of imagination and had no good ideas." He started several businesses that failed and had to file bankruptcy before finding success.

Albert Einstein was expelled from school, and Zurich Polytechnic School rejected his admission. Teachers told Thomas Edison he was too dumb to learn anything. He made a thousand unsuccessful inventions before inventing the light bulb. Michael Jordan was cut from his high school basketball team. Jordan knows success and failures. As he states in his Nike commercial, "I have missed more than nine thousand shots in my career. I have lost almost three hundred games. On twenty-six occasions, I have been entrusted to take the game winning shot, and I have missed. I have failed over and over and over again in my life. And that is why I succeed."

If you knew you could not fail—or didn't consider such opportunities as failures—what would you accomplish?

If these people allowed fear to control them, if they would have never known failure, they would never be the people they are today. Every life is filled with failure and disappointments. It's your reaction to those that allow you to be pushed back or pulled forward. So how are you going to react to your fear?

Fear asks you to believe something you can't see. Why not believe the opposite? You can't always see that either, so you might as well believe the positive as much as what your fears want you to believe. Why not believe you will succeed? That you'll get a standing ovation? You will find the love of your life? Your health will improve? Fear is believing the negative. Choose to believe the positive. You will find love. You will get that job. You will have a family. Believe instead of worrying. Believe and it will happen!

Don't hide because you fear the fear.

Be yourself.

**There is something that you can do
better than any other.
Listen to the inward voice
and bravely obey that.**

—Unknown

CHAPTER 21: *What's Holding You Back?*

You aren't living the life you want to be living; whether the reason is big or small, you aren't. Is it a relationship, career, family, unresolved feelings, not getting enough time to yourself, lack of self-confidence, finances, inability to envision your future?

What's holding you back? Is it money? No. Is it someone else? No. Is it fear? No. The only thing that is holding you back is YOU. I understand that you may think it is money, someone else, or fear, but it's not. It is only you. As much as you may not want to believe it, no one controls you but you. Someone else may manipulate, persuade, command, threaten, or ask you to do something. Only you control your behavior, attitude, mind, emotions, and actions. No one can make you do anything. So, what's holding you back?

We all have been through trials and tribulations. Everyone deals with problems. It's called life. Even people who seem to have the perfect life don't. They may not show you what's really happening in their world, but they have just as many issues as you. No one wants to scream their issues from the rooftops. People don't want to admit adultery, abuse, or drug use. They don't want everyone to know they can't have kids, pay their bills, or get a job. They don't want people to judge them. That is understandable, but no one has a right to judge anyone else.

When you acknowledge all the things that you try to sweep under the rug or ignore, you give yourself permission to feel. You free yourself from the burden that you've carried around with you for too many years. You realize that it's safe to let down the front you've continually put up, and by doing so, you allow people to know the real you. They will like you anyway. They will be able to identify with whatever you've been through because they have also dealt with issues.

At the tender age of nine, a stranger raped Cindy. Because of that trauma, and the reactions of shame and guilt by others, she felt isolated and alone. Eventually those events would take a toll on Cindy, destroying her health and happiness. It would take over forty years for her to ultimately find healing and joy.

She discovered that healing begins by dissolving the guilt, shame, and anger associated with adversity. Simple adjustments in thinking can eradicate such destructive emotions, which are a function of the mind, not the spirit that resides within every one of us. Using her life experiences and the skills that she learned during her twenty-four years as a corporate trainer, Cindy now offers to others an alternative approach to healing from any trauma, one that allows people to view life's tribulations as an opportunity for spiritual growth.

Known as The Joyful Survivor and author of *Awakening the Spirit: The Open Wide like a Floozy Chronicles*, Cindy specializes in mind-body-spirit healing and physical abuse recovery. Many people have praised Cindy for the way she has positively affected their lives, including Maria Shriver, who says of Cindy, "I know you will inspire others through your personal story of overcoming pain and suffering. I applaud you for having the courage and strength to share your extraordinary story."

There is no reason to be ashamed or embarrassed about whatever has happened in your life to make you into the person you are today. No one wants to scream her faults or mistakes from the rooftops, but you don't have to hide them, either. Like Cindy, you can use your story to inspire others.

Just like with any issue, people may judge you or think of you differently when they know your flaws. If you don't share your story, then other people who are going through difficult situations may feel like they are alone. If you help one person by telling your experience, then that's success.

Your issues or troubles don't define you. Those "bad" decisions don't make you who you are today. Did they allow you to learn about other people and yourself? Did you realize you are stronger than you thought? Now that you know, will you do better next time?

We all deal with multiple problems. If you think you don't, then you are either lying to yourself, accepting to ignore, or choosing to deny it. Stop living the lie. So what if you have problems? Life didn't work out the way you planned or expected. This is true for everyone. That's why it's called life. You can't predict what might happen. It's okay.

Come out from your hiding place. Admit what you've been through. Recognize you are just like the rest of us. You are not perfect! You have flaws. You have faults. Those don't define you; instead, they make you stronger. Change where you are going. Stand in the light. Embrace what you've survived. Ban together with others. Start by telling those closest to you about it. When you are ready, and you will know the time, make a real difference and tell people you don't know. You may be surprised how likable you become. They will identify with you, as you will with them. When you empathize with others' challenges, you let them know they are not alone.

When you share your secret about a "shameful" experience you've had, you will sigh with relief as the stress and suffering slide off your back. You will feel the release from everything you've kept inside. A new person will emerge, not the same old you who was merely living the fabrication of another—someone you aren't. Give yourself consent to stop living a double life. Look in the mirror and really see yourself for the first time. Your experiences will be new. Your perspective will be different. Your attitude will change. All because you give yourself permission to be who you truly are—the person who is trying to escape...the person who wants to be true... the person who wants to be free...the person you were always meant to be. Uncage her! Release her so that you can live your greatest life!

Stop living the lie. Tell your secret to others. It will free you!

ONLY THOSE WHO
RISK
GOING TOO FAR CAN
POSSIBLY
FIND OUT HOW
FAR
ONE CAN GO...

—T.S. Eliot

CHAPTER 22: *Risk*

Let's face it, most people don't like risk. Some might do just about anything to stay away from it. I'm just the opposite of this. I don't just sit there...I almost chase after risk.

1. Went bungee jumping (twice!) when it first became popular in the 1990s
2. Instead of going into Corporate America where I could have worked for years and made over six figures, I waited tables and went to grad school not knowing what I wanted to do in life.
3. Moved to Los Angeles without a job or knowing anyone—met one of my best friends there. Moved there a second time to get into the ridiculously hard world of acting.
4. Studied abroad in Norway alone, where people said I would be so depressed since there are only a few hours of sunlight each day in the wintertime—best decision ever.
5. Found my passion—glad I did it when I did.
6. Went skydiving—huge adrenaline rush!
7. Hosted a talk show, which started me on my path of helping people.
8. Traveled alone and learned so much about myself.
9. Earned three college degrees—I'm my biggest advocate.
10. Started a business—why not?
11. Volunteered in Africa by myself—had an epiphany.
12. Went shark diving—an even greater adrenaline rush than skydiving. I can't wait to go again.
13. Wrote a book and interviewed NFL players and The Biggest Loser contestants and a winner of the show—had a blast.

14. Wrote two more books.
15. Tried online dating—unsuccessfully, but at least I tried it.
16. Quit a job without a backup plan.

These are just some of the things I have done in my life when there was great risk involved, whether physical or emotional risk. Think of things you can do in your own life that will push your normal boundaries, especially in areas where you are risk-averse. I took advantage of the opportunities that presented themselves, and you can too! Don't be afraid of risk. There is great reward involved. If you don't risk, you never know what you might actually achieve.

Make a list of the things you have done in your own life where you had to risk something, whether it was a relationship, your emotions, finances, or your life.

What have you risked in order to live your greatest life? Be reasonable with this list. Don't put that you gave up one pair of shoes to buy another, or that you risked your health by letting your spouse cook one night. What have you seriously risked in order to live better, increase your experiences, or learn more?

Risk is a funny thing. People don't usually enjoy doing it, yet you don't know how far you can go or how far you have come until you risk something. When I look back on my list (which is written in chronological order), there were so many things that I didn't know how to do, but I learned along the way. If you want something bad enough, you will find a way to make it happen. You might have to ask others for their advice or help, but you will still succeed.

Think of all the things you have wanted to do but thought there was too much risk involved: asking someone out (fear of rejection); starting a business (didn't know how to; worried you wouldn't succeed); changing careers (not sure if you would like the new one); finding your passion (where do you start?); learning more about yourself (scared of what you have to confront). There are always things we don't do along the way for one reason or another. Don't let that happen to you. Take advantage of every opportunity, just to see where it will lead

Nelson Mandela, Oprah, Bill Gates, or Mother Theresa...
what did they do? What did they accomplish? None of them were
born into well-to-do families where life was just handed to them.
They created their own path. They had to sacrifice and stand up
for what they believed in order to achieve success. So many people
have to stand on the ledge and be willing to jump off the cliff in
order to spread their wings. When those people look back at their
lives, they see the risks they took. Some of the risks paid off, others
taught them lessons. They became who they are because they risked
something. Imagine what the world would be like if those great
people hadn't made their mark. Imagine how your world could
change if you were a little more like them—if you were willing
to take bold risks and make an impact on humanity. Think of the
people in your life and how they would be affected if you were
willing to take that one step forward; if you were willing to put
your toes over the starting line. What would their world and yours
look like if what you risked turned out in your favor?

You don't know how it's going to be unless you try. You may
not want to risk it because you're scared. You may be plagued with
the What Ifs: "What if it doesn't work?" "What if I fail?" "What
if it doesn't happen?" "What if I don't get that job?" "What if I
don't find the man/woman I dream about?" "What if the business
fails?"

Well, what if it does? But then again, what if it works? What
if you succeed? What if you get that job or person you want? What
if your business takes off and becomes the next Microsoft? Do you
think Bill Gates thought, *What if Microsoft doesn't take off?* No. He
probably thought, *I know this is going to take off. I absolutely know
THIS is the future.* With that level of conviction inside you, you
will move mountains. If you can imagine, *What if it doesn't happen*,
turn that around and imagine, *What if it does?* Think what your
world and your life will be like when you succeed. Stop thinking
negatively. Then, don't just *think* it will happen; *know* it will
happen. Once you know it, you will live it, eat it, and breathe it.
Then it can't help but come to fruition.

Refuse to take the easy route. Instead, take the path less traveled, no matter what others say. Don't let anyone talk you out of being you. Don't allow someone else—not even your parents, spouse or best friend—to tell you that you can't do something. If you're like me, you'll do it just to prove them wrong. Get out of the safe zone, step into the light, and you just might find out who you are truly meant to be.

Stop living so safely. If you are not risking things, you are not really living. Jump at the chance. Fly higher than you thought. Join the group. Ask her out. Get the job. Parachute out of the plane. Build the house. Risk and you will soon discover what it's like to truly live. You never know what you can possibly gain if you aren't willing to risk something. You don't have to risk everything; you just need to risk something.

You might get the career you want, the man of your dreams, or more blessings than you can imagine. If you don't take that leap, you will never know if you can fly. What are you willing to risk in order to have the future and the life you want? What opportunity are you going to take to find success financially, emotionally, and spiritually? What can you do to step out of your comfort zone? You will look back and see the distance you have traveled, the obstacles you have overcome, and the challenges you have conquered. You will have succeeded because you were willing to get out there and risk something. Take a risk; you will receive your reward! If you were brave today, what would you RISK?

You don't have to risk everything; just risk SOMETHING! Imagine your world when it pays off!

For a long time it seemed to me that life was about to begin-*real life*. But there was always some obstacle in the way, something to be gotten through first, some unfinished business, time still to be served, a debt to be paid. At last it dawned on me that these obstacles were my life. This perspective has helped me to see there is no way to happiness. Happiness is the way. So treasure every moment you have and remember that time waits for no one.

Happiness is a journey, not a destination...

—Souza

STEP 4: FINDING YOUR PASSION

CHAPTER 23: What Is This?

What does it really mean to find your passion? You may not have heard this term when you were younger.

LOST...have you ever felt complete and utterly lost? Have you ever had that feeling, when you look at yourself in the mirror and it's almost as though you are not seeing you in the reflection? You look at yourself as though you are watching a character in a movie, someone who is not you. There is no way it can possibly be you. Certainly, you wouldn't do that. You would never incur so much debt, let time pass without following your dreams, or put yourself on the back burner. When you hear of someone being in an endless job for ten years and hating it, you swear that you would never do that. Then before you know it, it is happening to you. You find yourself in the same situation you swore would never occur. It happens to us all. We don't think we are "those" people that bad things happen to, just to find out six months or a year later, the exact same thing we knew wouldn't happen to us is occurring.

It's easy to say that you are not that "kind" of person or that it would never happen to you. When, in fact, you don't know if it would. We all like to think that we don't make mistakes, have mishaps, and incur failures. But we do...and they don't make us who we are.

You too may feel completely lost. It's okay, because you are on your way to finding yourself again. You may have thought that would never happen to you. It's perfectly fine that it is. Acknowledge it and say, "I feel so lost. I may not know how to find myself or my passion, but I'm going to start right now." Now is your time to put *you* on the front burner...to invest in you.

When you don't know how to start something, how do you start? It would be easy for me to say, "Just change careers, find your love, get your finances in order, make time for yourself." But if you don't know how to begin, how do you do it?

Get out there and get involved. Go meet people. Your answers are not going to come to you as you sit on the couch. But when you are putting yourself out there, maybe you will meet a financial advisor who can help you with your debt. You might also meet your future spouse. Maybe you'll find an expert organizer to help you with time management. You might just be in the right place at the right time.

For many singletons out there, we wonder why we are still single or where the person of our dreams is. We go to work, come home, lie on the couch, and watch television. Then, *knock, knock, knock*, someone is at the door. I open it, and it's George. In a cute, innocent yet enthusiastic voice, I say, "Hi George (Clooney that is). I've been waiting for you (here on my couch)."

It doesn't happen that way. If it did, George would have shown up years ago. When we stay in our routine day after day, it's no wonder why we can't find someone. It doesn't have to be a future spouse; maybe it's a career, your passion, or financial security. Doing the same thing the same way will give you the same results you've always gotten. It's time to step out and away from that. Now is the time to do something different.

Opportunity will find you, but only if you get out there and be open to it. It will never find you if you stay at home surrounded by no one but yourself, hoping and praying it will knock on your door. Take a risk...get out there. So much awaits you. Be rebellious and take a risk today!

Be willing to ask for help. You might not know where to look or what to do, but there is always someone you know who does. People you know have interests and hobbies you may not even be aware of or they know other people who can help you. Your uncle may be friends with someone who is hiring for a new position. Your husband's coworker's brother may work for a debt consolidator. Your friend's boss may have a son who is single and looking. Post it on Facebook and ask your friends whom they might know. Just put yourself out there and you will be surprised at the responses you get and the number of people who are willing to help you.

Finding your passion is about igniting what's inside of you. Stop repressing your dreams and goals. Don't think you can't do it. Instead, say, "Yes, I can!" You will encounter people who push their doubts on you saying, "There is no way you will be able to get that job." Others may say, "Do you know how hard it is to open your own business? Yours won't succeed." Just because they aren't pursuing their goals doesn't mean you should have the same negative thinking to dominate your life. Don't listen to their limitations, and make sure you don't apply them to yourself. There will always be naysayers. They may have given up on their own lives, thinking their time has passed, but don't let them discourage you. You are meant for more. You have more talents than that job. You deserve to be treated better than that relationship you're in. You know you are worth more than that meager salary. Just like me selling copiers and fax machines years ago, when I was capable of so much more—you are more than that, too. You are destined for greatness.

Put aside your what ifs. What if I don't get the job? What if he doesn't like me? What if I don't make more money? What if I don't have the skills? What if I fail? The what ifs won't get you anywhere, and will only give you a lot of misery and worry. They don't exist. They are wasted energy. Take a stand and refuse to spend any time wasting energy. You only have time for positive thinking. You know you will get that job. You know you will find your love, live your dream, get that promotion, or succeed in business. When you know you are destined for greatness, the what ifs cease to exist. When that happens, you will find your passion. You may not know how you are going to do it, but you are going to find a way, because greatness won't wait, and you won't settle for anything less.

Don't know how to find your passion? Let us explore it together.

Feeling lost? Don't despair. You are destined for greatness!

Thank you for being.

—Seneca Greeting

CHAPTER 24: *Where Do You Find It?*

Finding your passion is about being honest with yourself. It's not about being a forty-year-old man still setting his sights on being a professional ball player. I definitely believe in dreams, but it's highly unlikely that's going to occur, for no other reason than he is (probably) past his prime pertaining to playing professional sports. Finding your passion is discovering what lies inside your heart. What would your heart tell you to do if your life wasn't filled with responsibilities? If money were no object, what would you do?

Sometimes we find our passion due to unforeseen circumstances, in the unlikeliest places, or because of something painful that we experienced in the past. Maybe you tried to commit suicide as a teenager and your therapist helped you through it, and this has inspired you to be a counselor. Maybe your child got hurt in a car accident, and now you find yourself an advocate of a cause such as seatbelt safety laws, or living joyfully and successfully with a permanently disabled child. Your passion can be found anywhere.

Dianne never would have imagined where she would find her passion. Here is how she tells her story:

"I awoke one morning and got up to start my day as usual, but as I walked across the room, I caught a glimpse of myself in the mirror. I was the same woman I'd seen in the mirror my entire adult life, but this time, I did not recognize her. She was frail, she walked slowly, and she had no expression of life in her face, but yet she looked familiar. I just could not place her.

"As I walked into the bathroom, it took all I had to muster up the energy to splash cold water on my face. Maybe then I could continue on with whatever this day (or should I say my husband) had in store for me. When I stood and looked in the mirror, which I tried not to do at first, it struck me like a bolt of lightning."

Dianne paused for a minute before continuing. "'Oh my god,' I whispered as a tear rolled down my cheek. That worn-out lifeless body of the woman I didn't recognize—all ninety pounds of her—was me. Tears began to flow; I could not understand what had happened to me. How did I end up like this? What had happened to the little girl who always believed in 'happily ever after'? Had life forgotten me? I was once a beautiful blonde teenager smiling as I dressed for the day. A touch of makeup here and there was just enough to let my happiness shine through. I felt I could conquer the world and be anything I wanted to be. After all, I had plans for a career and was the envy of all my friends because I had the best-looking boyfriend. I was so proud to be with him. Little did I know at that time he would be the death of my spirit and almost my life.

"At this precise moment, I heard a banging on the bathroom door accompanied by my husband bellowing, 'DIANNE!' Trust me, when I heard that tone, I didn't waste time. All I could do was jump to his command. I closed my eyes briefly and murmured, 'Why should this day be any different?' I told myself to just do what he said and maybe there would be no bruises today. But of course I was only kidding myself. When I was a teenager of sixteen, I never dreamed that dating and then marrying this man would have such an impact on my life. After all, he was the love of my life. It never occurred to me that when he questioned every move I made, I should have seen that as a red flag of danger. I thought he was just being loving and concerned about me, and that made me proud.

"I would not wish my marriage on my worst enemy. The first two days of married life were blissful, but then it happened. It was the first time that I felt actual physical pain from his so-called love and concern—and the first time I was introduced to his fist. Ask me now just how proud I am to have been his wife. I was ashamed to show my face in public and almost always hid behind sunglasses and long sleeves. I thought I was hiding it from the world, but the world knew.

"After the third day of marriage, my marital bliss was over. I was shocked and stunned. What had I done to make him so mad? Angry and hurt, I wanted to go home to my parents, a loving home where nothing such as this had ever happened. But then he stood there professing his love for me with tears in his eyes saying how it would never happen again; how could I not forgive him? After all, I was to blame for upsetting him.

"One night we went to church, which was unusual for him, and I walked up to ask the preacher to pray for us. Of course, my husband walked up right behind me so close I could feel him breathing on the back of my neck making the hair stand on end. All I wanted was to ask the preacher to pray for us. I had been taught that a wife should stand by her man, and that my Heavenly Father did not want divorce no matter what. But I did not dare say this to the preacher because then my husband would know what I had been thinking, and surely I would pay a severe penalty for speaking up once we got home. Quickly I changed my wording and said I wanted to re-dedicate my life to the Lord. As I hung my head, I knew that God understood my lie and why. After all, he had been protecting me. I was still alive.

"When we got home I was happy, and my husband seemed happy too, but that was short-lived. He ripped my robe off and started hitting me, saying, 'You only went up front to flirt with the preacher, and so other men could see you. How dare you!' Then he grabbed my arm and pulled me to the mirror. There they were again, those words he always spat out at me: 'Look at you,' he sneered as he laughed. 'Who wants that? Used property, that's all you are. You have four kids and you're nothing.'

"Then that day came when I knew it was do or die. And I mean literally **die** for me. I felt beat, worn down, and tired, and had no life in me at all. Had it not been for my four kids, I more than likely would have taken my own life just to get out of the hell I was living in. How could I even think of having a life, let alone a good life or a happy life? After all, I did not deserve it. I was not a good person or a good wife, and no one wanted me.

"That one **huge** step I took that day could have been the day of my death. It turned out to be the most rewarding day of my life and my children's life. On that day, I left and moved from Louisiana to Dallas just to get away from him. I was not prepared for any of it. But the thought that kept me going—even though I felt I did not deserve a new life—was that my four children did not ask for any of it. It was up to me to get them on a different road—to set their feet on a different path for their lives.

One day after moving to Dallas, I put on an actual **real** used suit that I had been given to wear to a job interview. All I could think was *Me? A job? Yeah, right…* I had no car, no money, and I felt as though I had nothing to give to any job. Thoughts of the past bombarded my head. Something literally led me to the pair of red heels in my closet that had also been given to me. I remember sitting on the bed to put them on, and it was almost like slow motion as I slipped my right foot into that red heel, the first pair of heels I'd worn in years. I distinctly remember how easily it slid over the heel of my foot and how perfectly it fit. I sat back for a moment, then crossed my left leg over and began to slip my left foot into the other red heel. When I stood up, I felt a tingling sensation from the bottom of my feet to the top of my head. My head went from looking down at the floor to being held high.

"As tears came to my eyes, I knew exactly what I wanted, and with help from my family, friends, and programs available to help women in my situation, I found a job and an apartment. With blessing from above, I went back and got my four children. We lived better than ever before. They found out what it was like to have food whenever they were hungry, to no longer have to live in the dark because now we had electricity, to hear a telephone ringing, and to have a car—yes, a CAR! For the first time in my children's lives, they were able to have things they had never had before.

"I lived in the Dallas area for about two years before meeting Roger, my wonderful husband. He was so patient and understanding with me; he had to propose a couple of times before I would accept. It was confusing to me to be loved and accepted for who I was. Here this man was telling me just the opposite of everything my ex-husband had told me. What did Roger mean when he said I was beautiful? What did he mean when he said he believed in me? He must be lying, because no one wanted me; my ex-husband always said so. But then one night there was this little soft tap on my shoulder as Roger was looking at me and telling me he loved me. I remember it so vividly. As I sat there thinking, *I do love this man*, a small beautiful voice said, *Dianne, this is not your ex. It's okay to love him.*

"So, once again, I raised my head up, just like that day when I put on those red heels, and for the first time in years I did something that I had not done in a long time: I smiled and believed. I decided to marry Roger, and here I am twenty-seven years later still happy and in love. Roger even adopted all four of my children with no contest from their birth father. All four children have nice homes and good, loving spouses. I could not ask for more. I have dedicated my life to reaching out to others and helping them see that people who care **will** help them. With the power I felt from those red heels and the sound of an angel's voice telling me that it was okay to love again, I know I can always draw on that strength that we're all given, deep in our souls, for the rest of my life."

Dianne started a movement, aptly named the Society of Women Who Love Shoes, whose motto and goal is *Healing one sole at a time*. After five years of testing and developing the concept in another city, she made the decision to form an official 501-c3 charitable organization. Their purpose is to support women and families of abuse by touching on something that is near and dear to so many women's hearts: shoes, and of course, fashion. The plan is to take this to the next level and possibly open a resale shop, a food pantry, and have clothes available to donate to women who can't afford to buy them.

Currently, the Society does monthly mixers with hundreds of attendees reaching into their pockets and closets to donate money and shoes to Dianne's cause. She plans to have an announcement party and a yearly gala.

Dianne never knew her trauma would lead to her passion. She was blessed to leave her situation alive, and she tells her story to encourage others in their struggles. She ignites strength in others and uses her organization to provide for people who, like her, have endured domestic violence and need assistance to begin a new life.

What is your passion? Does a prior experience play a vital role in your life? Do you motivate, encourage, or inspire people with your story? You, like many others, may not have this answer. You may be saying, "I've thought about that a lot, and I still don't know," as you shake your head in frustration. You might feel that everyone but you is living the life they want. They seem to have a job they love, in their field of interest, and they're living a blessed life. Rest assured, you are not alone. Many people are not in the career they love or their life isn't what they imagined. They might feel lost and unsure, not having the answers they so desperately want. They, like you, also don't know how to resolve those dilemmas.

Passion is not something that is tangible, and only you know when you have found it. You may love doing a particular thing and think you will want to do it as a job or vocation for the rest of your life. Then, when you start doing it, you realize it's not what you thought it would be or it doesn't conjure up the feelings you imagined it would.

Finding your passion is something that can only be felt with the heart. When you're passionate about something, the more you do it, the more you want to do it. The more you want to do it, the more you know you can't live without doing it. You can't imagine a single day when it won't play a role in your life. You don't have to eat, sleep, and breathe it…but you will want to. When you find your passion, you can't imagine doing anything else in life. And your world, without it, would be dimmer, less lively, and almost as though you weren't really living.

Your passion becomes so much a part of you that you aren't sure where it ends and you begin. It is engrained in every ounce of you. It fills all your molecules, pores, and crevices. You are filled with joy just thinking about it.

It's not a job. What's the difference between a job and your passion? A job is something that pays the bills. You might even like your job, or at least not hate it, but that doesn't make it your passion. You don't have to start your own business to find your passion. You can work for someone else as long as what you do exudes from everything in you.

Jacob is a marketing professor for graduate students. Each new semester when he introduces himself to his class, he says he doesn't work a day in his life. He loves what he does, and so it is never work. If he didn't get paid, he would still teach.

How can you find your passion? Think of something you love so much that if you didn't get paid to do it, you would still do it anyway.

Get passionate. Isn't that what life is for—to get excited about everything? It doesn't matter how big or small it is, be passionate about a variety of things. That's how life should be. What is your passion? The difficult part comes when you have no idea what the answer is. You don't have to rush to find it either. It will come in time, as so many things do.

Give it some thought. It's more than what you like or love. I love chocolate, but I wouldn't want to spend several hours a day eating it or working with it. What is your driving force? Why do you get up in the morning? You have to have a reason to get out of bed and face the world; what is it? Is it to make sure you fix a healthy, balanced breakfast for your family? Do you fight for the disease that took your sister's life? Do you run so it doesn't take yours? Do you wonder what you will learn today or what you might teach others?

Do you love flowers, sports, or talking on the phone? Do you find yourself not finding the right style, size, or fit with clothes, and that inspires you to take on this challenge? Are you wishing others were concerned as you are about bullying, eating disorders, or mental illness, and know how to ignite that spark in them?

Write down all the things that interest you, whether only slightly or a lot. Beginning with the first moment in your day, take notes about everything you enjoy, from the coffee you drink and the soap you use to the outfit you put on. You might even come across your passion at the job you hate. You might think about it while sitting in traffic on the way home. You might do some great thinking in random places and at inopportune times, like right when you are trying to fall asleep, when you first get up in the morning, when you're in the shower, while driving, or at the store. Keep pencil and paper everywhere—on your bedside table and in your bathroom, car, and purse. Don't find yourself in a predicament where you are trying to dig up any kind of scratch paper, receipt, or business card in your purse on which to write down the brilliant thought or idea you've just had.

Then take all your ideas and review them. How can they turn into something more? How do they translate into a purpose? Whittle down your list from the things that interest you the least to those that interest or intrigue you the most. Those are your top five passions.

Next, ask a friend what your three best strengths are. How do her answers contribute to your list of ideas? How can you use them to discover your ambitions? Her answers should compel you to brainstorm ways to turn your passion into a goal.

For example, if you love running and your friend says you are dedicated, motivated, and love helping people, you can start a company that makes specialized running shoes. Maybe you will want to work for Susan G. Komen and begin new Races for the Cure internationally. You may want to be a personal runner or triathlon athlete, participating for those who can't do it themselves.

There is passion inside of you; be willing to explore it. You will eventually find your way to the answer. Don't let someone else tell you that you shouldn't follow that passion, and don't let anyone lead you to believe there is no way you can turn your passion into a moneymaking venture. With enough persistence, perseverance, and personality, there is always a way!

Constantly take notes to explore your passion. You never know what you'll find.

The purpose of life is
to live it,
to taste experience
to the utmost
to reach out eagerly
and without fear
for newer and
richer experiences.

—Eleanor Roosevelt

CHAPTER 25: *Don't Do This*

So many people decide some guy is good enough for them even if he isn't. They resign themselves to thinking they aren't worth anyone better and tell themselves, *Oh well...he'll do.* Or they don't really like their job, but they stay in it for their entire lives just for the sake of security. At one time or another we have all settled.

Maybe you knew a certain guy wasn't right for you, but you stayed with him for a few years anyway. Or you despised your job, the environment, and your boss, but you were there longer than you care to remember. We put ourselves in situations that we don't like, hang around people who aren't good for us, and work at jobs that drag us down, yet we allow ourselves to stay in these situations way past the time we should have moved on.

We tell ourselves, "It's easier than finding another job." You might say, "This person is really not *that* bad. I could do a lot worse." You may even try to convince yourself that you don't deserve better. The truth, however, is that you absolutely, definitely *do* deserve not only better, but the best—meaning, the best for *you*. Don't tell yourself this is the best as you can get, because there is better!

Karen had just started college when she thought she'd found her future husband. Being in her mid twenties, she had been in enough relationships to know what she wanted. Initially, they were really happy, and so they moved in together.

After about a year, Karen knew things were spiraling downhill. He drank so heavily some nights that he would black out, leaving Karen to clean up any messes he left. He had problems at work, which caused him to drink even more once he got home. When Karen confronted him about his drinking, they would fight.

Karen began to hate going home, never knowing what she would find or who he was going to be that night. She knew in her heart that something wasn't right. She wanted and deserved better, but she didn't know what that was or what it looked like.

It had now been three years. He was supposed to be the man she was going to marry. She didn't want to give up that image—that dream.

They talked about him changing, and he agreed to do so. And he did, but only for about two months. Then he went back to his old ways. Finally, Karen took a stand and said, "I can't take this anymore," and she left.

She hadn't given up too much of herself during those three years, but it had been enough to make her realize she refused to do it any longer. It was time she regained control of her life. She wanted that image and dream she had in her mind, and she knew that *this* guy was not the right one for her. The heartache and hurt was almost unbearable, but she didn't want to give up. She wouldn't give up on herself.

Have you ever been locked into this kind of relationship? You knew that you deserved and wanted more, but for some reason you were unable to pry yourself free. You somehow became addicted to the relationship while losing yourself in it. Even if this is all you have ever known, you *know* are worth more than that. Better is out there even if you haven't experienced it.

Sometime later, Karen started seeing someone else who really opened her eyes. In the short time she spent with this new guy, he showed her the definition of better. He treated her like she deserved to be treated by opening doors for her, giving her flowers, and taking time to have meaningful conversations with her.

He demonstrated what *better* really meant. Once she had experienced that, she knew there was absolutely no way she was going to settle for less, ever again. That thought wasn't even in the realm of possibilities. She had always known she wanted more than what she'd had in her previous relationship, but she didn't know what that entailed. What did it look like? Now she had experienced it, and back stepping wasn't an option.

People who settle in life have a hard time finding real happiness. It seems they know in their hearts they have settled; they always want more, and they know they deserve more. Yet they choose to "make do" with less. Why do you want to make do when you know you can have more of what's best for *you*? You may be saying, "Jessica, my life is easier by having this guy in it, even if I know he isn't really meant for me." Yes, that may be true. He might help you pay the bills, take care of the house, and provide for your kids. Does that give you satisfaction? If you are not happy with him, then the benefits don't outweigh the cost. He might help you, whether it's financially, emotionally, or physically, but if there is something missing, you know what you need to do.

"Jessica, that makes life harder." I understand that, but life is not meant to be easy. That's why it's called life. No one's life is easy. Too often we look at celebrities, movie stars, or singers and think, *I wish I had her life.* I know I used to think that. It seemed as though they had it all—looks, glamour, fashion at their fingertips, perfect careers, and great relationships. Why couldn't I have all that too? Then I started thinking more about it: cameras following them everywhere, without a moment of privacy; people scrutinizing them for gaining five pounds or their clothes fitting differently; magazines telling half-truths about them or even their loved ones.

Imagine you're making a quick trip to the grocery store. You are starving because you didn't have time to eat lunch. Since you have to take your daughter to ballet and son to soccer, you know dinner is still a couple hours away. You grab that candy bar you've been craving for two weeks or that small bag of chips. Suddenly, out of the corner of your eye, you catch someone watching you through a camera lens as you are licking your fingers from the smudged chocolate of the candy bar. Snap, snap, snap. He has just taken pictures of you at the worst possible time.

A month later you are in the grocery store, glancing through a magazine as you wait in line at the checkout. You notice it's a picture of you: Your hair is in a messy ponytail, you're wearing your workout clothes, you don't have any makeup on, and what the heck is that? You are licking chocolate from your fingers.

You guessed it: you—the celebrity you—no matter where you go and what you do, cameras are following you. You can't just jump out of bed, throw on some old clothes, and quickly tie up your hair in a ponytail to go run errands. You have to be decked out to the nines in case cameras follow you, even to the dang grocery store. Who wants that? Do you want to grab coffee or gas and have someone waiting to take your picture? I know I don't. You would lose all sense of freedom. You would never have a moment of peace; you would be looking over your shoulder every two seconds. So yes, they are celebrities. They are famous. People idolize and want to be them, but they also have less freedom and liberty than you do. They are criticized and ridiculed, yet they still choose to be in that line of work because they love it—because they can't live without it. It's their passion. They wake up each day wondering how they can help others through their work, and with that comes a price. They can't imagine doing anything else in their lives. A few may do it for the notoriety, but most of them do it because it is what's in their hearts. They can't *not* sing; they can't *not* write; they can't *not* explore the world of fascinating characters through their acting career. And their life would not be complete doing anything else.

Do some people have it easier than others? It may appear so, but there are things you might not know about their lives. They may be suffering from a devastating loss, health issues, or family turmoil. They could have been in the field for twenty years before they caught their "big break." Things are not as simple as they seem, and there is always more to a story than what is told to the public.

Don't settle. Be done with complacency. Leave mediocrity. Go after your dreams. You are closer to them than you think. More than that, you deserve to strive for the best, because no one wants to go through a settled life knowing they are greater than the life they are leading. Whether it's with your relationship, career, passion, or dreams, don't settle. Follow your heart; it will never steer your wrong.

Don't settle for less than the best in what you deem important. You deserve only the greatest!

The only people for me are the **mad** ones,
the ones who are mad to live, mad to talk,
mad to be saved, desirous of everything at
the same time, the ones who never yawn or
say a commonplace thing, but
burn, burn, burn,
like fabulous yellow roman candles
exploding like spiders across the stars...

—Jack Kerouac

CHAPTER 26: How I Found Mine

When I graduated from OU, I had no idea what I wanted to do in life. I didn't even know how to find the answer. After a few months selling copiers and fax machines, I realized without a doubt I was in the wrong job. I still didn't know what I wanted to do. So what else could I do?

I went to grad school for about a year to bide my time while trying to figure things out. Really, I was trying to figure myself out. I decided to move to Los Angeles to look for a marketing job in the entertainment industry. After a year of waiting tables, I moved back to Texas because I couldn't find another job that was more meaningful to me. A couple months after returning, I was working at an advertising agency when I got laid off. I had been thinking about returning to grad school, and this was my prime opportunity to do so.

While in grad school, I still didn't have a direction for my life. Although I was majoring in marketing, I had long ago thought, *As much as I like marketing, I just can't picture myself doing it for the rest of my life.* I wouldn't settle for working at a job fifty hours a week for fifty years hating every minute of it. I didn't want to look back on my life and wonder what I had been doing the whole time. I refused to do that.

Although I didn't know what I wanted to do, I could tell you what I definitely did *not* want to do. I figured it was the next best thing to knowing what I wanted. I narrowed down the list as best as I could. In the meantime, I took random classes that interested me.

Even though I can barely draw a stick person, painting intrigued me. I wondered if it was possible to paint well even if I couldn't draw.

I didn't know, but I wanted to find out, so I took a painting class. I found my own impressionistic style, and to this day, I love painting.

I also took a few acting classes. After the first one, I caught the bug. I was interested in acting and decided that once I finished grad school, I would move to Los Angeles to act. And I did. My roommate knew the producer of a talk show and suggested I have my own show. I never considered having a talk show and wasn't even sure what I had to say. The more I thought about it, I knew that even if I didn't have much to say, there were a lot of people out there who did. So I started my talk show and my passion was ignited. I eventually realized that I didn't just want to be a host on television, though. After two years on Los Angeles cable television, I moved my show to Texas. I wanted to learn all the facets of having a talk show. I wanted to know how to produce, direct, edit, and shoot. I learned it all and earned a third degree, another bachelor's degree, in broadcast journalism.

After pitching my show to executives in Los Angeles and Las Vegas, I had a decision to make. Talk shows are the most difficult format to sell, even with celebrity hosts. If they get picked up, most fail. Many people don't know this little known fact about talk shows. I know I didn't. People in the entertainment industry don't want to take a chance on talk shows because they are so risky.

After hearing from several executives about the difficulties of selling a talk show, I didn't know what to do. I had spent seven years and obtained another degree, all for my talk show. I could either keep going down the path I was on—producing, directing, shooting, and editing my shows and then uploading them online while waiting tables to pay the bills—or I could take another direction, though I was not sure what that direction would be. I was confused, especially since I thought I had found my passion.

I unintentionally stopped looking for show guests, but in the meantime, I got another idea; what about writing a book, a memoir about my dating life? With that one thought, I started my first book. While I was writing it, my thoughts evolved. The more I contemplated my life, the more I realized there were lots of things I had experienced that I could share with others to help them navigate life. I also thought about guests I'd had on the show and what I had learned from them.

There was no conscious or rational thought about becoming a public speaker. It was as though the idea was placed in my head, and I knew right then that helping people was what I really wanted to do.

While I researched public speaking, there was never a moment of uncertainty. I instantly knew I would speak about how to Live Your Greatest Life. From the moment I started speaking, the light shone down. I knew, without a doubt, I had found my calling, my mission, and my purpose. I wanted to do whatever I could to help people find their true purpose and live a better life, the life they were meant to live. I wanted to help them be the person they were meant to be and give them the tools to reach their potential. I wanted to help them attain greatness, whatever that meant for their unique lives. My career as a life coach was born.

I had heard the terms calling and purpose, but I really didn't know what they meant. Even now, it's difficult for me to explain. It's not something that can easily be put into words; it can only be felt. When you find your calling, you will know it. If you are asking yourself if something is your mission, then it probably is NOT! When you have found your mission, you will have no doubt. You will feel it in all that you are. How will you know? Your heart will tell you. And when you find your calling, you will have found your purpose, too, and it will align with your passion as well. These three—calling, purpose, and passion—go hand in hand. My passion is helping others. My calling is to help others though coaching, speaking, writing, talking, videos, workshops, and seminars. My purpose is to help you Live Your Greatest Life.

> Your calling, purpose, and passion go hand in hand. How can I help you in your life?

If you are going to doubt
something, doubt your limits.

—Don Ward

CHAPTER 27: *The One Four-Letter Word*

Have you ever considered the word "can't" and all that it implies? It's only four letters, but it can change your thoughts. When you change those, you change your outlook on life, thus changing your world in the process. **C-A-N-'-T**: I can't do that. I can't achieve that. I can't fulfill my dreams. I can't climb that mountain. I can't beat this disease. I can't find my passion. I can't find the man of my dreams. I can't reach my goals. I can't be who I want to be. I can't, I can't, I can't...

Those four letters can and will keep you from doing anything. That one word will keep you from being who you are meant to be. It will prevent you from reaching your potential. It will allow you to remain exactly where you are without your even realizing it. It will stop you from doing, being, reaching, fulfilling, finding, and exceeding. It will be exactly what you allow it to be. If you don't give claim to it, then it won't have the power over you. Take back your power and say, "I C-A-N..." Now make it a complete thought and say, "I can do it!" I can find love. I can achieve success. I can find my dream career. I can exceed any limitations placed on me. I can accomplish my goals. I can have a family. I can conquer my fears. I can be a leader. I can do whatever I set my mind to.

The difference between **can** and **can't** lies in that one letter T, which makes all the difference in your thoughts. When you change the way you think, you change your actions. Negative thinking will keep you from doing everything. If you keep telling yourself you can't, you will give up on yourself before even attempting the task. When you use positive reinforcement by telling yourself you can, you will find yourself truly believing it, and you will achieve the desired results. When you think you can, you are more willing to take the leap to try it. When you try it, you realize that all you need is to believe in yourself and success will follow.

Take wine for instance, someone has to feel the grapes, perfect the combination of grapes, and taste the wine throughout the process from winery to consumer. If you have a nose and taste for wine, that someone could be you.

After you have gone through the steps of writing down your interests as discussed in Chapter 24, take time to explore your answers. You need to really contemplate these ideas on a deep level. Think of all the jobs that relate to the field you're interested in, from the behind-the-scenes jobs to the ones at the forefront. Dig deep and research what type of careers you can have pertaining to your interests and passions.

For example if you have always wanted to play professional ball, your dream of being involved with sports is still alive. You may not be able to play pro ball, but you can be a coach, personal trainer, physical therapist, or a sports videographer. If you love having gatherings at your house, you can be an interior designer, decorator, event planner, party planner, wedding planner, meeting planner, or home organizer.

If you enjoy cooking, you can sell your own food, establish your own line of cookware, write a cookbook, create a site for recipes, start a cooking networking group, or be a host for a cooking show.

You might be a parent whose greatest source of joy and fulfillment is parenting. You can start an organization for parents (infants, toddlers, stay-at-home moms, multiples, five kids under five years), create a blog specializing in worries of new moms, start an advice column (what every parent should know/do/say), design a maternity or kids' clothing line, or invent a new item every parent/child needs. There a million things you can think of pertaining to being a parent or having kids. They teach you something every day; what are you learning from them that you can share with others?

Think creatively and brainstorm. There are a variety of different jobs in every field that you might never have considered, and it just might be that for one, being self-employed is the key. Maybe you were meant to form your own business and provide jobs to others. There are no limits to what you can do when you break your thinking out of the usual nine-to-five rut.

If you watched season six of "America's Got Talent," you may recall one of the contestants, who had been diagnosed with cancer. When she was given this news, she couldn't dance anymore. Instead of sinking into depression, she created a technology called Iluminate. When the stage is dark, she controls the lights from her laptop as the dancers perform. Lights cover different parts of the dancers so that only those specific parts ignite when she types in the code to her computer at given times, creating a type of special effect. For example, a long pink light could be on the dancer's arm. When she wants the arm to show, she types in the code that lights up the arm. The lights change from arms to legs to head to feet and between dancers, so that it is all completely in sync, appearing as a flowing show. It's an amazing presentation. The creator said that if she had not gotten cancer, she never would have created the technology because she still would have been happily dancing and not thinking about anything else.

Who would have thought a dancer would develop technology? She was probably more surprised than anyone to learn she could do this, but quite often, when limitations are placed on one aspect of your life, your creativity abilities can spring forth in another. Expand your thinking and dig deep to discover what talents and abilities you have that can translate into a career you can create for yourself, or a business you can run, or a service you can provide others. You may improve technology that changes the world. You may create a new position for yourself, and then establish that type of job in businesses all over the country (this is especially true in the field of digital media). When you allow your mind to break free of limitations and not be confined by the molds that others want to put you in, anything is possible. You never know what career is out there for you. Allow yourself the freedom to be crazy…think outside of your comfort zone. You may just find out who you are truly meant to be.

Dig deep to think of careers that interest you, and if you can't find such a career, create it! Explore outside your comfort zone.

Every great dream begins with a dreamer.
Always remember, you have within you
the **strength**, the **patience**, and the **passion**
to reach for the stars to change the world.

—Harriet Tubman

STEP 5: FULFILLING YOUR DREAMS

CHAPTER 28: *What Does This Mean?*

Fulfilling your dreams: what does that constitute? Does it mean that everything will be as you imagined? That life will be perfect? You probably had a dream of some kind when you were younger. Whether it was to be a rock star or to find your Prince Charming, you had a dream. What was it? Did you want to walk on the moon, own your own company, or have four kids? Did you make it happen? Are you living it now? Most of us aren't. Somehow life got in the way of our dream. We watched as our dream slowly faded into the background, and now we can't even see it there.

We are so busy getting our kids to after-school activities, working at a company that doesn't appreciate us, and taking care of the house, we don't even know how to start finding our dream again, if we even remember what it was.

Your childhood dreams may be lost, but you don't need to have those same dreams. After all, you aren't the same person you were when you were eight years old. Fulfilling your dreams is more about creating dreams and watching them come to fruition. If you could do anything in the world, what would you do? If you could go anywhere, where would you go? If you could meet anyone, who would it be?

In order to fulfill your dreams, you need to know what they are. What does your heart say? What have you always wanted to do, but you don't think you have the time, money, or resources for it? You do. If you wait until you have more time, more money, more resources, you probably won't ever do it. Now is the time to do what you've been putting off. You've always wanted to go to Australia, so go. You've wanted to play in a band; go find a band to join or start a band yourself. Don't know where to look? Ask around. Google it in your area. Look on craigslist.com. There are plenty of ways to make it happen. Find a way to do it. Stop analyzing and over analyzing it. Make a plan. Set a goal. And if you can dream it, it's possible.

What in this life would make you the happiest? Make it happen! Want to drive a Ferrari but can't afford to buy one? Go test drive one! Want to know what an adrenaline rush feels like? Go scuba diving or just dive off the high dive board at your local pool. Can't have kids, but want to be a mom? Look into adoption or being a foster parent. There are a lot of kids out there who need your love. Find a way to share it with them.

Do you want to start your own business but feel like you don't have the resources? Call another entrepreneur and ask to meet with him or her for fifteen minutes (and keep it to fifteen minutes unless she says she has more time). Find out how she got started in her business. What trials and tribulations did she have to endure? How did she overcome them? What advice would she give to you? Ask her if she has time to become your mentor. How did she get financing? You might be surprised by the people who are willing to help you; you just simply need to ask them. Women enjoy empowering other women. People like talking about themselves, and they want to help others. Just be willing to ask.

You can go to your local SBA (Small Business Association) and ask them for resources, advice, and help with your business. Millions of dollars in grant money is not distributed each year. Apply for a grant to get your business started. If you are a minority, there is even more money available for you.

Fulfilling your dreams doesn't necessarily pertain to your career. It could mean you want to better provide for your family. How can you do that? How can you have more time to spend with them? Do you leave work at 7 pm instead of 5 pm? When you get home, are you on the phone with someone, talking about work instead of focusing on your family? Do you watch football on Saturdays or

Sundays instead of spending time with your spouse (unless he/she enjoys watching it with you)? Being able to better manage your time will help you achieve greater success. You will have more time for enjoyment when you arrange your priorities. Don't spend your time at home thinking about work.

What will it take to get your finances in order so you can take a much-needed vacation to where *your family* wants to go? Do you need to learn how to better budget your money? Many people make enough money, but they don't know how to budget. They spend $25 a week at Starbucks or $60 on a Friday night eating out when they owe $15,000 on their car or have $20,000 in credit card debt. Is that you? Are you frivolously spending your money even though you are in debt? You can get your finances aligned with your future by seeing a debt consolidator.

Maybe fulfilling your dreams pertains to finding love. What are you doing to achieve it? Are you getting out there and meeting people? Are you asking your family and friends if they know anyone who might be compatible with you? Lily told Ariel she had just broken up with her boyfriend of two years. Steve, Ariel's husband, had a brilliant idea. He wanted to set Lily up with his best friend, Troy. Ariel and Steve had known Lily and Troy for years and never would have thought of setting them up, especially because Lily had always had a boyfriend. When she broke up with him, though, Steve saw an opportunity without Troy even asking him. So the four of them went on a double date together. Troy and Lily hit it off, and now they are going out together. The perfect person for you is out there, but you have to seize the opportunity or it will pass you by without your knowing. Don't be afraid to ask around. You never know who knows whom.

Take a little time to look inside yourself. See what's missing in your life. What have you always wanted but somehow forgotten about in the mundane rut of everyday life? What is your heart craving? Go out there and get it. You will have to spend some time and possibly money to make it happen. But if it's in your heart, be persistent. Dreams don't become reality easily...but with perseverance, they will happen. Keep making strides forward. Push toward your goals, because, yes—your dreams can come true!

What's your dream? Make strides each day to make it happen!

FOLLOW YOUR DREAMS TRANSFORM YOUR LIFE

—PAULO COELHO

CHAPTER 29: *How to Do It*

As with anything, living your greatest life starts by taking the first step. Don't talk yourself out of doing it. Dreams take time to be fulfilled. With each day, you are taking a step. You are either taking a step toward your dream or away from it. Where did your steps take you today?

I understand how there are days when you want to be lazy. You want to sit on the couch and watch television, and you're lucky if you move to get something to eat. I get it, because I've had those days myself. Yes, you need those every now and again, but the key is to limit them. If you are doing this twice a week, that's not every so often. Soon that twice a week will double, then it will become the whole week. Before you know it, you will be lucky if you move toward your goals once a month. It just so happens when this route is taken, years pass by, and you wonder how you got to where you are. You think about the past year, and you can't believe how the time has flown by. It wasn't *that* long ago when you were actually doing something pertaining to your dreams. What you are doing *now* keeps you exactly where you are—and it is not the place where you want to be.

So, how do you achieve your dreams? Think differently. Don't be confined by others' rules. There are a million ways to go about solving one problem. Begin by doing research into whatever interests you. Google it, go to your library, or ask a neighbor, friend or coworker for help. Find one person out there who is doing or has done exactly what you want to do. Want to buy your first house, have a successful marriage, or start a non-profit organization? Let your fingers do the walking and discover who has done it. Then schedule an appointment with her, and if you can meet with her in person, even better. Pick her brain. Ask her how she did it. Get her advice, suggestions, and help. Ask her, "What do you wish you had known when you started?" Learn from others' mistakes and successes. Who knows? You might end up exactly where you want to be.

Regina wants to start a non-profit organization to educate the public about bullying. A girl at her daughter's school is a bully, and the principal refuses to take action, even though four girls have complained about the bully. Because of the consequences we're seeing today, such as the victim's suicide or accidental death, Regina doesn't want to see another child suffer. As she brainstormed how to form her non-profit, Regina talked to friends about the concept. Several people told her how difficult it was to start a non-profit, get funding, and learn the business aspects.

There will always be people trying to persuade you against your calling. Don't let them. Don't allow their negative thoughts even scratch the surface of what you want to accomplish. Put your hand up to them and say, "If you aren't going to support me in what I'm doing, then I don't want you to be a part of it," and walk away. You will get plenty of naysayers. You don't need your friends and family to be those people. If they are, expunge them from your life, no matter the difficulty. When you know in your heart that you are meant to do something, you need to only surround yourself with supporters. Having those Positive Pollys around will make all the difference to you. Because yes, there may be difficulties, and things may not go exactly as you had planned, but that's the case no matter what you do in life, so you might as well follow your heart and do what you love.

I have had plenty of those experiences myself. It's actually a running joke with my family and friends. They know things can never go as expected, so I say, "Welcome to Jessica's life..." Things can never be *that* easy in it. But I've learned some amazing lessons along the way, and I wouldn't trade that for anything. When things don't go as planned, the last thing you want around are Negative Nancys. The Positive Pollys will pick you up, make you laugh, and give you a dose of reality…and that's exactly what you will need. They will also keep you focused on your goal and reasons for doing what you are doing.

Don't let anyone talk you out of what you want to do. There will be time to have the responsible job. There is time for you to meet him. You can do that another day. Today is the day you need to take that audition, jump out of a plane (with a parachute), or jet off to Vegas at a moment's notice. Take a risk. It may be the exact risk you need to take to change the rest of your life!

Don't let anyone talk you out of what you want to do. There will be time to have the responsible job. There is time for you to meet him. You can do that another day. Today is the day you need to take that audition, jump out of a plane (with a parachute), or jet off to Vegas at a moment's notice. Take a risk. It may be the exact risk you need to change the rest of your life!

Talk show host Janee' Harrell knows how difficult it can be to take a risk. There will be people who tell you that you can't do it. She says, "When you are an entrepreneur who is charting new territory, it takes unimaginable perseverance to succeed." Having been a motivational speaker and television personality, Janee' was willing to put her name on the line to fulfill her passion. She knew that using media to share hope was her calling, and she wasn't willing to give up on that belief.

She knows that in order to achieve your goals, you must be willing to take a risk. She says, "Anything is possible if you only believe and never, never quit."

Getting a signature show on a major network isn't easy, but Janee' found the strength she needed to accomplish this goal though her faith in God, her belief in her dreams, and her friends' faith in her.

The Janee' Show is the first of its kind in the Dallas/Fort Worth area with a focus on walking women through life's journey. Janee' doesn't just talk about it; she risks putting herself out there, too, allowing viewers to experience her life, flaws, disappointments, and successes along with her. She will show you what goes on behind the scenes of the journey, exposing herself and allowing you to see the real her. Now that's a risk that will absolutely pay off. It's a risk to show your authentic self, but people will like you more for it.

Listen to yourself. Only you know what is right for you. When people tell you to give up, listen to what your life is saying to you.

Don't limit yourself, whether it's time, expectations, or goals. Know you can do and achieve anything. You may say, "Jessica, I've been doing this for five years, and it still hasn't happened for me."

If it is in your heart, have faith and know it will happen for you. What if you stopped and then the next day, everything came to fruition. Your day is coming. Know that if you stick with it, then all you desire will be your reality. I didn't give up with my talk show; my life and my path led me in a different direction. Listen to your life. It may be leading you to a more fulfilling way. Don't be so stuck on what you want that you forget to listen to yourself. Watch for detours that may surround you. You will be guided to where you need to be. Make sure you pay attention to the signs in your road.

Most importantly, don't give up on yourself. Things may not happen the way you want them to. They may not happen in the time you want them to. But know they will happen. They will happen when they are supposed to happen. You may not be ready for it. Maybe you need to learn a lesson or two before they do. If you know you are ready for the man of your dreams, he might not be in the right place for you. If he isn't ready and you come into each other's lives, things won't progress the way they are meant to. If you are not fully prepared to handle the job you want but you get that job anyway, you might sabotage your chances for promotion, thus keeping you stagnant in the future.

Your dreams will come to fruition. Never let someone talk you out of them. Be true to who you are. Listen to your life. Be patient. Don't give up. You will prevail!

Listen to life…it's speaking to you. What's it saying?

Promise yourself to be so strong that nothing can disturb your **peace** of mind. Look at the sunny side of everything and make your **optimism** come true. **Think** only of the best, work only for the best, and expect only the **best**. Forget the mistakes of the past and press on to the greater achievements of the **future**. Give so much time to the improvement of **yourself** that you have no time to criticize others. Live in the faith that the whole world is on your side so long as you are **true** to the best that is in **you!**

—Christian D. Larson

CHAPTER 30: Get Rid of Anchors

What is weighing you down? Is it a dead-end job or relationship? Is it your perspective on yourself? Do you have Negative Nancys in your life? You need to get rid of everything that is tying you down in one way or another.

Life whispers to you. It comes in the voice of, "That's strange..." or, "That doesn't seem right..." or, "Can that be so?" When you don't listen, it talks a little louder with a shove or a thump. Then it will be a brick thrown at you. Finally, you will be hitting a brick wall. Some people need the brick wall to finally pay attention, when they should have been listening to the whispers. We make all kinds of excuses when we don't want to hear what life is whispering to us. We say, "I must have misunderstood," or, "He isn't really like that," or, "It's not going to be that bad." We could save ourselves a lot of heartache and pain if we would walk away when we know something isn't right for us.

The longer we stay the more we will get hurt. This is demonstrated when we hit the wall and end up on our bathroom floors, wrapped in only a towel, crying because it hurts so much as we ask ourselves why we let it go on for so long. We wonder how it got off track or how it could end this way, when all along the signs were telling us loud and clear that this is exactly where it was going to end up. We just put on our blinders, as we sometimes do, so we can enjoy ourselves one more day, which turns into another year or two. Then we have the nerve to ask ourselves how or why it got to this point, already knowing the dreaded answer.

When you allow someone or something to prohibit you from being who you are meant to be, attaining your goals, and reaching your potential, you are allowing that person, experience, or situation to control you.

It is difficult to walk away when you are tied to someone emotionally, but I know you can do it. You have to look after you! No one else is going to do so. You have to pay attention to what life is telling you. Are you listening?

Whether you have been with that person or in that situation for two days, two months, two years, or twenty years, if it's not right for you, then it's time to get out. You may say, "That's easier said than done." But really, it's not. We make things more difficult than they really are. Tell yourself to get out of it, and then do it. Give yourself no excuses or reasons for staying there. It's easy to do that. But haven't you already done it for too long? You know in your heart it's not right for you. You know you need to just walk away. Take the first step toward the door. Don't look back. The next step will be easier, then the next and the next, and it will become easier with each stride until you hear the door closing behind you.

The only thing stopping you from getting rid of your anchors is you. Yes, when that day comes, it will be rough. The next one will be the toughest. The first week will be hard, but once you've reached a month, you will have achieved a milestone. You know you need to leave...you need to run. You have been there way too long, and it's time to think about yourself. What do you want? Where do you want your life to be? If you don't release yourself from that person or situation, you allow them to capture your hopes and dreams. You are giving up yourself for them. Why are they more important than you are? They aren't!

You deserve respect and to be treated better. You deserve to make more money, to be loved, and to be taken out. You deserve it all! And you can have it as soon as you get rid of the anchors weighing you down.

In order to move forward and have the life you truly want, you have to find your inner strength. Realize it, then know it! Realize enough is enough and then *know*, without a shadow of a doubt, that enough is enough. Whether you are addressing a significant other, boss, family member, or friend, no matter his response, you will end it. Don't let him talk you into staying. You will walk away. You will get out of the very situation you swore you would never be in. You don't have to be mean or a jerk about it. You can say, "I need _____ (fill in the blank with respect, love, care, communication, promotion). You do not give this to me, so I must end this and walk away." You do not owe him anything, but you do owe yourself everything. Don't just think this; know this. You owe YOURSELF everything! Get rid of the anchors, because once you do that, you free yourself. You are liberated to be exactly who you are meant to be. You are empowered to reach all you are destined to reach. You are greatness and you deserve nothing but greatness. Your journey is just beginning!

You owe yourself everything. Don't just think it; KNOW it!

EACH OF US HAS A FIRE IN OUR HEARTS FOR SOMETHING... FIND IT AND KEEP IT LIT!

—Mary Lou Retton

CHAPTER 31: How to Balance

What is the secret to balancing your home and work life? It's more than just dividing your time between the two. It's about balancing you against everything else.

Think of it like this. You are holding a board with both of your hands. On the right side of the board is a picture representing you. On the other side are small action figures (representing your kids and significant other), business cards (work), stuffed animal (your pets), can of food (cooking), sponge (cleaning), and a piggy bank (finances). This side is the everything/everyone else side. So, just to clarify, on your right is a solo picture of you and on your left is everything else. Now, imagine you must walk across an eight-foot by three-inch balance beam (the journey of life) while holding this unbalanced board, making sure you don't drop any of the things on it. Oh, and you are in heels (for guys, you are in cleats) to represent that life is never easy, and you must complete this walk in five minutes or less.

Do you feel nervous? Are your hands shaking? How slow are you walking? How well are you doing? Does anything fall off? Do you lose your balance and stumble? Do you successfully make it across, ten minutes after you started? That's how we feel going through life. Little do you know, you get halfway across the balance beam and it curves, because the journey of life is never a straight path. Just when you thought you are walking through life perfectly and you couldn't imagine things being any better, life throws you a curve ball. How quick are your reflexes? Can you duck and adapt? Or do you get hit and are down for the rest of the game? Life brings its share of ups and downs and winding roads. You must overcome obstacles and trials, but even if it takes you longer than you expected, you still manage to get through it.

You may fail in some aspects, but you learn from those experiences. You might fall off the balance beam, as we all have at one time or another. How fast did you get back up and onto the beam? Did you lie there for a while, not sure what to do, licking your wounds? Or did you jump up and say, "What's next?" Those tumbles help make you who you are. They teach you necessary lessons and build your character. Whether you stumble, trip, and fall down, make sure you get back on that balance beam.

Now imagine you have finally made it to the other side of the balance beam. You turn around, and now, on the right side of the board with the solo picture of yourself, you add vitamins (for health), a small silver boat (traveling), a book (reading), a book of Sudoku puzzles (for challenging your mind), and foot lotion (spa pedicure). Now that you've begun to prioritize, you realize that you can rearrange some of the items on the left side of the board, the everything/everyone else side. These can now find a different place in your life. You move the can of food and spouse action figure toward the middle. Then you rearrange the child action figures and stuffed animal to the outside. When you have help with the everything/everyone else side, you carry a lighter load, so you can take off the piggy bank. Again, don't be afraid to ask for help.

Now both sides should be more even, and the board a little easier to balance. This time when you walk across the balance beam, you might be moving faster. The board seems a little lighter. You walk with grace and ease because your load isn't weighing you down so much, and it is not unevenly weighted on one side.

Prioritize your everything/everyone else side and give yourself more time. This doesn't mean you have to neglect other responsibilities. It means that you need to enjoy some time resting, relaxing, reading a book, soaking in a bath, meditating...whatever it is you love to do, without interruption. If someone is bugging you or the phone is ringing during your "me" time, then it doesn't count. If you need to schedule this time in your day the same way you would an important meeting that you cannot miss, then do so. You need to take time for you. It will make a world of difference to yourself, and to your sanity. You can't effectively take care of other people or situations without putting yourself first. You may accomplish the task, but it will take you longer, be more difficult, or not get done properly without taking care of you first. With this time, you are able to balance yourself—mind, body, and spirit. When you are balanced, you are able to fully participate in other aspects of your life, which makes everyone around you happier.

> ## You should always be your number one priority. EVERYTHING else comes after.

Risk
more than others think is safe,

Care
more than others think is wise,

Dream
more than others think is practical,

Expect
more than others think is possible.

—Cadet Maxim

CHAPTER 32: *Become Proficient in Time Management*

You may say, "Jessica, it's easier for people to go after their dreams if they don't have a husband or kids to take care of." The truth, however, is that it doesn't matter what responsibilities you do or don't have in your life. What matters is your level of commitment and the passion that resides in your heart. If you and another person were taking steps toward similar goals, your days may look completely different. You may wake up an hour earlier and the other person may go to bed an hour later. She may be able to attend a networking function at night, while you take your kids to their activities. Her schedule may be more flexible and yours more structured. Don't let excuses crowd your thinking and tell you that you *can't* do something. If it weighs on your heart and is important to you, then you will find a way to make it happen.

You have to work with what you have, and you have a lot. See the openings and opportunities of how you can accomplish your goals. For instance, when you are waiting for your son to finish his shower, you could be writing your presentation or making phone calls. When you are in the waiting room at the doctor's office, you can be doing research on your laptop or cell phone. How quickly and how well you accomplish your goals and dreams has everything to do with time management. Take whatever time you have, whenever you have it, and continually work toward fulfilling your dreams.

Do you wake up with just enough time to get ready for work, and then find that you run out of time every morning? Even if you woke up ten minutes earlier, would you still be rushing to get to work on time? If you find yourself frequently thinking, *I never have enough time*, know that you have just as much time in a day that everyone else has. She manages to run a successful company, and he has plenty of time with his family. How is it you have trouble making dinner and getting your kids to their activities on time? We all have responsibilities we need to fulfill in a given day, but lack of time management and organizational skills keep us from accomplishing them.

Time management is a key factor in much of our lives. Do you wait until the last minute to do things and then you constantly rush around to accomplish them in the allotted time? Do you have a "To Do List" that just keeps growing? How can you better organize your time daily, weekly, and monthly?

Are you ever in the middle of doing something when you have to get up for some reason, and when you walk by the television, you get wrapped up in whatever show is on at the moment? You then find yourself an hour later trying to get back to what you were doing previously. I know what it's like for my attention to go elsewhere. I have to pull myself away and say, "Jessica, why are you watching this? This is not important. You need to be writing." I know you might be saying, "Jessica, I need to wind down after working all day. I need some time to unwind." Everyone needs some down time, and I'm all for that. But I'm also for it when you *have* the time. Don't say you don't have the time and then spend two hours catching up on your DVR. Spend those two hours being productive, even though you just spent all day at your day job. Keep the television turned off if that's what it takes. Watch your shows in small increments online and on your schedule. Making your dream a reality isn't going to happen overnight. In most cases, it is like having another job. So when you are done with your bill-paying job, you will most likely have to go home and work on your dream, your goal, your passion—whatever it is you want to be doing full time. This shouldn't feel like work. Since it's your passion, you should want to do it.

When you prioritize, make sure you leave adequate time for each task but not too much time. Too much time allows you to get distracted toward less important things. Think about the things you dread, whether it is cleaning, cooking, or research. You get online to conduct research, but you open up a window for your email, another one for Facebook, and yet another one for Twitter. Instead of doing your task, you are spending most of your time on those social sites, which takes away from time with your family.

Make sure you get the things done in the time you have allotted yourself. Don't find yourself watching your favorite shows first. Then it will be late, you will be tired, and you will go to bed before even starting what you should have finished. Television, game playing, or shopping can wait until you have finished your priorities. Otherwise your things-to-get-done list will be so long, you will feel like you can never catch up and are constantly chasing something. None of us enjoys feeling as though we're sinking and the sand is caving in around us.

Do you ever feel frazzled, as though you're running to and from pointlessly, never really getting anything done? You feel as though you have a million things to do and not enough time. When you are constantly rushing around, panicking as the clock ticks the hours away so quickly, you feel like a zombie just going through the motions, not even paying attention or remembering what you just did because time is controlling you. You are under its possession. Don't let it control you. Prioritize and manage your day to fit in the necessities of your dreams.

Otherwise, when you are barely able to stay afloat, you may just give up and stop working toward your goals altogether. That's the last thing you want. Don't ever give up on your goals and dreams. When you do, it's as though you've given up on yourself. If you give up on you, others will too. And no one deserves to be given up on. You are destined for greatness. Keep taking strides toward it! It's closer than you think.

To keep from slacking off and falling behind, I make sure I do my priorities first. I contribute to what is important to my dreams and me. I encourage you to do the same. Even if you don't accomplish all that you want in any given day toward the fulfillment of your dreams, make sure you put forth the effort to do at least something. Even if you don't think it's worth it because the task may be something small, like sending out an email, do it anyway. You may get a reply from it tomorrow that could change your life. Do ONE thing each day to move toward your dreams!

If you feel as though you don't have enough time to accomplish what you want, consider hiring someone to help you with your organizational skills. In the same way that some people need help getting their desk organized, some people need assistance with their time management. It takes practice to be efficient with your time. Don't be afraid to ask for help. If people get help to learn about computers, how to run a company, or to become a better singer, you should be willing to learn more about how to wisely manage your time.

Since time is the one thing we can't get back, be willing to seek training to increase your skills. Become an expert in organizing your time. At the end of the day, you will find you have excess for doing what you want to do. It will increase your productivity at work or in your business. Improving your time management skills will carry over into helping your significant other, kids, coworkers, parents, and friends too. You will have more time for them and be more productive in all you do.

> Do one thing each day toward fulfilling your dreams. Become an expert in time management.

Go confidently in the direction of your dreams!
Live the life you've imagined.

—Thoreau

CHAPTER 33: *Commitment*

Do you ever want something for someone so badly that you want to just do it for her? Do you wish she wanted it as much for herself as you want it for her? Well, that's how I feel as I write this. I cannot make you do these steps. I cannot make you want to have a better life. I can't make you know that you deserve better. I cannot give you the motivation, passion, or commitment to make it happen for yourself. If I could, I would.

I want you to see all the greatness you have ahead of you in life. If you get past this hurdle, there is so much beyond it. You've seen how wonderful your life can be. You've imagined your world with a better job, your finances in order, an improved relationship, and more passion in your daily life. Now, it's up to you to follow through in order to make your dream life a reality.

Many kids love activities, sports, games, or band. In time, they may find they just want the end result. They want to play in the games, attain the highest level, or be first chair, but they don't want to practice in order to get there. Some adults have the same approach to life. They don't want to do the work. They just want the end result (make more money, have a dream job, find love, lose weight), but they don't want to put forth the effort. It doesn't work like that.

I can give you the steps. I can tell you the techniques. I can help you increase your skills, but I cannot make you take action. Even if I could make you, I wouldn't want to.

I want you to want this, although I know the initial thought toward achieving your greatest life may be difficult or overwhelming at first.

No one likes looking for a new job, even if it's her dream job. The thought of having to do the searches, then applying, waiting for an answer, and hoping to be called in for an interview is enough to make anyone give up before starting. This is without even thinking about the actual interview process itself. No one enjoys this. But it's a necessity to be doing what you want to be doing: to be working in an inviting, welcoming, encouraging environment and for good pay. You might be looking for better upward mobility, promotional opportunities, or flexible hours. Or you may want one doing what you truly love and are meant to do. The process isn't inviting, not to mention getting the job, learning their methods, acclimating to the new environment, and becoming familiar with your peers and boss. That is a frightening process, especially because we all want to be liked, and we have no control over how well we will be received.

Even though starting seems scary or intimidating, the end will make it all worthwhile. You will be doing what you love. You will feel as though you fit in. You won't have to deal with the hostility or lack of support at the other job. You will feel as though you are in your element, and that you've finally found where you are meant to be, doing what you are meant to be doing. That, my friend, will make all the difference in the world. All of the other things involved in this process, such as getting your resume updated, buying a new suit for the interview, dealing with sweaty palms during the interview process, will just wash off you. You can see the image. You can picture yourself already at the job.

Then, when you're sitting at your desk, in the corner office (because no matter where you start at this new company, you know your final destination is the corner office), you think back to when you first started knowing if not for accomplishing the simple tasks of the application process, you would not be here. You would not be able to look out over the city from that exact location. You would not be making money to not only provide for your family, but to save for their education, your retirement, and your leisure activities. You would be possibly struggling not only to pay your bills but to stay positive and keep your sanity at the same time.

It starts in the pit of your stomach, makes it way up your esophagus, through your mouth, and before you know it, you're smiling. One that comes deep from the inside, not just because you're sitting in the corner office, but because of one thought: that because you believed in yourself and knew you would succeed, you have accomplished that in every way imaginable and then some. You have more than you thought possible, more than you could have imagined because you never wavered in knowing it would happen.

When you are determined, you will not let anything or anyone stand in your way. Even balancing your life and time management will become easier when you have the commitment to do so. You will find the time to spend on you, because that's what needs to be done in order to achieve your goals. You will find the time to make things happen, whether it's working for two-hours on achieving your dream after you've come home from your paying-the-bills job or going to school at night. You will rearrange your priorities to accomplish your goals, knowing you shouldn't wait any longer.

No one can stop you; you are that laser-focused. When someone says, "No, I can't do that for you," you find someone else. When a manager says, "No, I don't have it in my budget," another company will have the money. Rejection is never easy, in any capacity, but it's part of life. Look at rejection as a blessing. Thank goodness it didn't work out with them, because someone better is in store for you. Don't spend your time on rejection, because you won't be able to see the opportunities that await you if you do. Use your energy and efforts on the doors opening for you.

Don't do it halfway unless you only want half the results. Put everything you have in it, everything you are, and everything you believe. Give it your all and then some, and expect nothing less in return. If you aren't getting the results you want, and you know you are truly putting all your energy into it, then maybe what you're doing needs to be tweaked. Ask other people their thoughts or suggestions. They will probably have an idea that has never occurred to you. Have them review what you are doing. A new set of eyes will give you a different and much needed perspective. They will likely pick up on something you haven't even noticed.

Whenever I have my younger brother look at something for me, he always comes back with a few suggestions. Most of the time, they never entered my mind. I love this about him, and it's why I seek his input. I know I can always count on him to give me his honest feedback. I also know it's going to be to the point, not rude or abrasive, and insightful. Ninety-nine percent of the time, I use his recommendations. I respect what he has to say. Find someone you admire or respect and have them give you advice. It will ignite you to go even farther in your pursuits than you might have gone on your own.

There is a better life waiting for you, and you have all the power in your possession to make it happen. When you believe this, when you know this, nothing will be able to stop you. Your desires will become your reality!

Be fully committed to living your greatest life. You have to truly want this for yourself!

We do not remember days...

we remember moments.

—Cesare Pavese

STEP 6: ENJOYING THE MOMENTS

CHAPTER 34: Being Present in Your Life

We spend so much time thinking about how we want our lives to be, whether it's wanting more money, a better relationship, a bigger house, a nicer car, kids who will listen, improved health, or a different job. When we spend our thoughts and time wanting more or wishing things were different, not only are we wasting energy, we are also not allowing ourselves to live in the moment.

I was volunteering at the Byron Nelson golf tournament, which is held every May in Irving, TX. I had just recently quit my hostile work environment job and started writing this book, not knowing what else I was going to do. I met several older men, and although they had been volunteering for years at this event, they made me feel right at home, joking around with me and giving me a hard time.

Jerry and I hit it off. Although he physically looked nothing like my grandfather, Jerry's personality reminded me of him. He made me feel a part of the group, even though he didn't know me. Feeling included is important, whether you're volunteering, at school, or at work, or with your in-laws, friends, or co-workers. We all want to feel included and liked. It's human nature. This same group of guys had been volunteering together, and close friends, for more than twenty years, so for them to include me as though I was one of their own meant a lot to me. It was like I had known them for just as long.

There was nothing holding Jerry back from his humor or his questions. He quickly asked me if I had a boyfriend. I said, "No, but I'm looking if you know anyone." So it became a theme over the next few days for us to be on the lookout for any potential men for me. At one point, I gave him a hard time about something, and his response was, "And I wonder why you don't have a boyfriend." We both laughed.

We didn't find a boyfriend for me in those few days, but Jerry gave me a great idea. After hearing I was writing a book, he asked me what it was about. I told him, "The title will be Live Your Greatest Life. More specifically, it's about discovering who you are, exploring what you want, uncovering your fears, finding your passion, and fulfilling your dreams."

Then he said, "And enjoying the moments in life."

And with that, this section was born. I then thought about all the things in life that we do, and how we often forget to truly enjoy them. We tune out. We are constantly looking ahead: waiting for the end of the day so we can go home, looking forward to a vacation, a birthday, the holidays, anticipating or dreading a certain phone call, wanting for summer to end or eagerly waiting for it to be here. How often do you really spend time in the present, in the moment, right now? When you think about it, you may be surprised at how little you live in the moment. Do you constantly look at your phone to see what calls or texts you have missed? Are you thinking about something else when your friend is talking? Do you look at the clock ten times in five minutes, wondering how much longer it's going to be until...? What can you do to be fully present in your life? What do you need in order to enjoy your days, your time, and your moments?

How often are you tuned out? How can you become more present?

Life is not measured by the
number of breaths we take,
but by the number of moments
that take our breath away.

—Unknown

CHAPTER 35: *Enjoying the Small Things in Life*

We've all heard the saying, "It's the small things in life..." You may not know until you are there, but when you know you're time is ending, what will you likely remember? Thinking about it this way may be easier. What did you get last year for your birthday? Christmas? Can you remember what you got?

The memories we hold on to are stored not only in our minds but also in our hearts. Does it matter what house you live in or what car you drive? Do you try to keep up with the Joneses?

When you finally reach them, they've moved on to something else. So it will always be a cat and mouse game, with you never being able to catch them. Why waste your time, money, and energy on this never-ending quest? You aren't doing it for you. You are doing it for appearances or for the persona that you want people to think is you, all the while knowing it's not really you.

Don't get me wrong. We all like to have nice things. I love clothes, shoes, and accessories, but I'm not going into debt to have them. They shouldn't be a priority in your life. Do you find yourself spending $30 or $40 dollars at a social event and then the next day regretting it because you now have credit card debt? That $40 would have been better spent on paying down the interest.

Many of us don't have the money...the actual money. We say we have it because we put it on a credit card, which gives us the *illusion* of having it. Meanwhile, we aren't paying off our credit card balance each month. We roll the balance over and over and over, so we end up paying almost double for the item once we add interest to the credit card. If this sounds familiar, why do that to yourself? You don't need the item. No one cares but you that you have it. It certainly won't matter to your real friends what you have or don't have.

Live for yourself, not for someone else. Don't allow someone else to "make" you feel as though you need a nicer car, a bigger house, a larger TV, or expensive clothes. When you spend money that you don't have, you are creating more issues for yourself and definitely more stress. You add the pressure of getting the money to pay off those unnecessary things. Then you want more things and then the stress increases. You will never catch up, and you will drive yourself crazy trying to. Enjoy what you have. Live the life you love by doing what you love, not by having more things, because things can't make you happy.

It's not about the material things in life; it's about lying in a hammock with your loved one, watching the stars, or watching your son score his first goal. These moments are priceless. Finding the love of your life is not about the flowers, cake, or a multitude of bridal arrangements. It's about watching her walk down the aisle toward you and knowing you can't imagine your life without her in it. The birth of your child is an event that can never be replaced. Remember taking that much-needed vacation with your family, the one where things seemed to go wrong from beginning to end? You look back on it later and have a good laugh at how much fun it was, more fun than if everything had been perfect.

You see him from across the room, your eyes meet, and you both just know you are meant for each other. How did you meet your spouse? Have you received a card, poem, or note that touched your heart, made you laugh, or brought tears to your eyes? These are the moments and events in life that are important. Start replacing the material, non-important things in life with these moments and times that really matter. How can you get more of these in your life?

What would happen if you gave up most of your material items? Could you be happy? How much could you give up and still be happy? How much importance do you place on your possessions? What if you could only buy clothes from a thrift store, or only purchase a second-hand car? What emotions would this conjure up? What value do you place on brand names or designer labels? Do you put too much emphasis in them? Does your happiness depend on having the best, most expensive things? If so, why? What does that mean?

Greta grew up very poor and had a difficult childhood. As an adult, she buys a lot of unnecessary things. It's as though the more things she has, the more she feels loved. Things don't have feelings. They can't love you. Having more of them won't fill the void in your life. It won't make you happier. You will just keep accumulating things but still feel empty inside. Then the cycle will continue, even when you don't want it to, because you won't know how to stop. These things are just holding you back. They are keeping you from experiencing the truly fulfilled, happy life you could be living. Let go of all the things, and then you will be able to let go of everything—people, situations, excuses, hurt, pain, or whatever is keeping you from living your greatest life. You will be able to release the ropes that have tied you down, set yourself free from the anchors, and uncage who you are truly meant to be.

When you are able to do that, you will be able to live in the moment. You will enjoy the time that is here and now. You will be in peace without that inner voice nagging at you. You will be able to let go and focus, even if for brief moments at a time, on yourself and your own happiness. When that happens, you will be on your way to living your greatest life.

How can you get more
enjoyment out of the small
things in life?

It's not the
years in your
life that count.
It's the life
in your years!

–Abe Lincoln

CHAPTER 36: *Work to Live or Live to Work*

How many hours a week do you work? Do you stay longer than necessary, because your boss hasn't left yet and you feel as though you cannot leave until he does? I understand why so many employees feel obligated to do this because they don't want to get in trouble for leaving earlier. I don't understand why companies have this unwritten rule. Some workers are more efficient than others, yet they get punished by having to watch the clock when they should be at home. How many needless hours are spent at work after the work is done?

On the other hand, there are people who won't pull away from work no matter what their responsibilities are outside the job. I understand how being a doctor would require unpredictable hours. But there is no reason why, unless you are in a similar career where life and death is on the line, you should sacrifice your home life for work. Too many people are working fifty to sixty hours a week, and it needs to stop.

Teresa works this much on a regular basis. She knows she needs to stop because it drains her every day, yet she keeps doing it. She makes good money, but she isn't really living life. She has a dream and isn't pursuing it. It seems she is living to work and not working to live. Her boss has told her she can leave at 5:00, yet she still doesn't. Her job is so demanding that it's difficult for her to leave when there is so much work she still has to do.

The work will be there tomorrow. Theresa has to learn to pull herself away, yet she doesn't know how. She has a pre-teen daughter at home who is involved in extra-curricular activities. If she can't leave work on time for herself, then she needs to do it for her daughter.

The more time she spends at work, the less time she is at home attending to her daughter. If you have kids and you refuse to leave work even when you know it's a detriment to them, then you will never have a "good enough" reason to stop working so much. If your kids are not a "good enough" reason, then nothing will ever be.

There will always be something that needs your attention or some project that needs your help. You and your family are your priorities; stop treating work like it is. Stop worrying so much about work and what you "need" to do there. Start worrying more about home and who needs you there...who wants you there.

Let go of your addiction to work. When you look back on life, you won't think, "I wish I spent more time at work."

You will however think, *I wish I spent more time at home*, or, *I wish we had taken more family vacations*.

Break free! Stop letting work dictate your life. You have the strength to make the change. You have the power to rule your own life. Get your priorities in line. Put you at the top of the list, and you will feel like you have gained a completely new life!

Don't let work control you. Set yourself free and get a new lease on life!

the adventure
of life is to learn.

the goal
of life is to grow.

the nature
of life is to change.

the challenge
of life is to overcome.

the essence
of life is to care.

the secret
of life is to dare.

the beauty
of life is to give.

The joy
of life is to love!

—**William Arthur Ward**

CHAPTER 37: *The Plan*

What's your plan for life? Are you living your life the way you planned to? Are you doing what you always thought you would do (or wanted to do)? If so, are you happy doing it, or would you rather be doing something—anything!—else right now?

Maybe the current plan for your life is not what you are destined to do. Don't spend so much time looking at your plan that you don't take the time to see another opportunity slapping you in the face. That's what happens. Opportunities whisper, and then they knock. If you still don't hear them, they slap you. If that doesn't get your attention and you don't stand erect at that point, it may never happen again. Why waste the opportunity? What is the worst that can happen if you take a chance and follow it?

When you jump out of a plane, you pull the strings to your parachute. What happens if your parachute doesn't open? You crash. The same thing happens when you don't take advantage of an opportunity. You will crash. Opportunities are there for you. Walk through the door and start living your amazing life!

Sometimes we focus so long on what we want that we are unable to see that may not be what we are *meant* to do. We see straight ahead with blinders on and a myopic viewpoint. Maybe where we are supposed to be is over to the right and not straight ahead. HE may have another path in mind for you. Stop ignoring the opportunities that come your way. Take a chance and grab them. They might lead you exactly where you want to be.

Are you familiar with a kids game called MASH? It's a pen and pencil game, laid out like this:

MASH

Boys   Age   Honeymoon   Bridesmaids   Cars   City
——————   ——   ——————   ——————   ————   ——————
——————   ——   ——————   ——————   ————   ——————
——————   ——   ——————   ——————   ————   ——————

Kids   Best Man   Ring Bearer   Flower Girl
————   ——————   ——————   ——————
————   ——————   ——————   ——————
————   ——————   ——————   ——————

Marks: IIIIIIIIIIIIIII

Across the top of the page write category titles for the areas of your life where you hope your wishes and dreams will come true. Then, put blank lines in columns under each category. Fill in the blanks with names that correspond to each category. For example, under the category labeled *Boys*, you would write the names of three boys you want to marry. Then you would fill in the other blanks with three answers according to their categories. One person would take a turn and close her eyes while the other would make marks at the bottom of the paper. When the one making the marks said, "Open your eyes," the one whose eyes had been closed would count the number of marks and cross off an equal number of names until only one item was left in each category.

Did your MASH dream, at the age of eight, become your reality? If your MASH dream didn't come true, are you still waiting for it to happen?

Are you focused on something you wanted when you were eight and haven't been able to give up since then? Make sure you want it for the right reasons. Do you still want the car that you wanted when you were young? Focus on more important things than the material items. Why do you still want it? It's not about the car; it's what the car says about you. Is it a status symbol? Will having that car let you feel like you've "made" it? Are you trying to prove something to yourself by buying that car? That you're self-sufficient or independent? You grew up poor and now you have money? Although it might *seem* like it's about the car, it isn't about the car. Deal with the underlying issues of wanting that car.

Are you still holding on to the dreams you had as a child? How can you alter those to fit your life now? Don't hold on to the past, but if a dream is still weighing on your heart, there is a reason for it. Ask yourself what that reason is. How can you rectify it? What steps do you need to take to fulfill your dream? How has your MASH dream played into your reality?

As we grow, our dreams take on different shapes and sizes. Your MASH dream may still exist, but make sure it's there for the right reasons. Maybe you have a song in your heart, and you've always wanted to be a singer. Life got in the way, but you never lost sight of that voice. You don't want to die with that song still in you. Now is the time to let that voice be heard.

Follow your heart; it will never lead you astray. But don't focus on your childhood MASH dream for so long that you forget to be open to the opportunities in your life now. That MASH dream may not be what's destined for your path. There may be bigger and better things in store for you, and if you focus too long on MASH, you will miss out on where you are meant to be. Stay true to who you are and you will find the right path for you.

Don't let your MASH dream dictate your reality. Stay open to other paths.

*Watch with glittering eyes
the whole world around you,
because the greatest secrets
are always hidden in
the most unlikely places.
Those who don't believe in
the magic will never find it!*

—Ronald Dahl

CHAPTER 38: *Absorb Everything*

Life is meant for living, but it's more about the experiences we have that make life worth living. Think how your life would be if you didn't have any experiences or if nothing ever happened to you. What would that be like? What meaning would your life have? How would that make you feel? Would you feel empty...lost... alone...forgotten?

It really doesn't matter if I'm at a fine dining restaurant or Babe's Chicken in Roanoke, Texas. I've spent very little money or none at all at places where I've had some of the best times of my life and eaten some of the best meals I've ever had. We get so caught up in our daily lives, between working, taking our kids to activities, or cooking that we forget to really enjoy our time. We are too busy talking on the phone or texting to soak in all the moments.

I remember one special time in particular because it was my birthday. My little sister, Jasmine, took me to lunch, and her husband, Sebastian, joined us. We went to our usual soup and sandwich shop, Boo Boo's in Arlington, Texas. If you are ever in the area, you must try their Cheese Broccoli soup. Open only weekdays, they have a great half sandwich, soup, and drink combo.

Since we really don't see each other often due to our work schedules, our conversation started out as any other. How are things going? What's new?

Jasmine and I are a lot alike, yet we are so different. She rarely talks about her life or shares stories of what's going on, and I'm the opposite. Yet our sense of humor is similar, and we tend to like the same things. Usually, when we get together, it's her eating and me talking. Then she comments on how she is almost done with her food, and I'm just getting started. So I stop talking, and she says a few things so I can eat.

Since Sebastian was there this time, he contributed to my usually one-way conversation. Jasmine and I are typically out of the restaurant in thirty minutes, but we were so engrossed in talking, we stayed one and a half hours. Jasmine then offered that we get dessert at our favorite Dairy Queen, so the three of us continued our conversation there.

When Sebastian parted from us (he had come separately), Jasmine and I continued talking. We had met up in a parking lot and driven to the restaurant together in one car (our usual routine), so we returned to that parking lot so I could get my car. When we arrived at the parking lot, we sat in Jasmine's car chatting for a few minutes, and for the first time in a long time, I really *saw* Jasmine. She was telling a story, and her eyes welled up. She allowed herself to be open and vulnerable, and although I know my sister, this showed me a side of her that I'm not used to seeing. I loved it. I loved knowing she trusted me enough to open up and show her true self to me.

As I drove off, I replayed the last few hours in my mind. I hadn't spent a single penny, but I knew this was a day I would never forget. There was nothing else I would've rather done on my birthday or no one else I would have rather spent my day with than my sister. No amount of money, activity, or job could outweigh the laughter, talk, and tears from the conversations of this one special day with my sister.

You don't have to be doing anything earth shattering to enjoy the moments you have. Are you talking on the phone instead of watching your son's soccer game? Are you texting while your daughter is at dance class? You just missed his goal or her solo.

Are you focused on whatever it is you plan to do next instead of being fully present in a conversation? I've been guilty of that myself, where I have tuned someone out because my mind is elsewhere.

Cherish the time spent talking over a meal, lying in front of a fireplace, or watching a sunset. Absorb it. Breathe it in...

Make a commitment to be fully present. This doesn't mean just listening. Take everything in...use your senses. What do you see? When you are sitting across from each other at a table and no one is talking, really look at the other person. See what you have never seen before, although you've seen this person a thousand times. Are you just noticing a small scar or maybe a mole you didn't know was there? Discover something new about this person who means so much to you.

What do you hear? Listen to her voice inflections, or how she smirks when she says a certain word. Maybe you've never fully appreciated her laugh, or how she tilts her head to one side the longer she laughs.

What do you feel emotionally and physically; is it more joy than you thought possible? Maybe you have goose bumps, because you are cold.

What do you taste? Are you drinking sweet tea like usual? Maybe you can't get enough of the chips and salsa you are eating.

Do you smell someone else's perfume in the booth next to you? Is something burning?

Take time to really enjoy the moments. Absorb them with everything inside of you. Stop thinking about the argument you just had or what work you need to do tomorrow. Give yourself the freedom to be in the moment right now, not concentrating on what already occurred or what has yet to happen.

When you decide to not live for now, you are doing a disservice to yourself. You are missing out on opportunities and times to be engaged. In five years, you won't remember a text message, but you will remember how you felt enjoying every moment of your child's first concert.

Stop limiting yourself. Give more of yourself. Be more actively present in all that you do. Don't be doing one thing and thinking of something else. Give all of you to what you are doing right now. If you are thinking about something else as you read this, you will have to go back and re-read it to understand it and fully grasp the depth of this message. What happens when you miss your son's first goal or your daughter's ballet dance? You weren't fully engaged, and you just missed it, because you just HAD to take a phone call, respond to a text, or whisper something to the person next to you. That precious moment is gone. You can't get an instant replay of it, and even if it's being recorded and you watch it later, it will not be the same, because you'll be filled with regret that you didn't experience life, in the moment.

Don't lose focus on what's really important. Commit to being fully present and completely engaged. Take time to enjoy the moments. When you do so, you will be energized by life.

> # Be fully engaged in all you do… you'll remember those moments for years.

THE **BEST** AND MOST **BEAUTIFUL** THINGS IN THE **WORLD** CANNOT BE **SEEN** OR EVEN **TOUCHED**. THEY MUST BE **FELT** WITH THE **HEART**.

—HELEN KELLER

CHAPTER 39: *Find a Way to Give of Your Time and Talents*

What is your purpose? How are you making a difference? Instead of thinking of life with the "get, get, get" mentality, contemplate the "give, give, give" way of thinking. The more you give the more you will get.

My best friend Lacy and I were meeting in Joplin, Missouri. She was driving from St. Joseph, Missouri, and I was driving from the Dallas/Fort Worth metroplex area. It was a nine-hour drive for me that seemed to lull in the middle.

I hadn't seen the reports on the news of the damage from the massive tornado that had barreled through Joplin, but I knew that the area had been hit. I was in the city, yet the main street I was traveling on looked as though it hadn't sustained much damage. I thought, *Okay, Lacy, why did you want to volunteer here? Nothing really bad has happened.*

I drove another two minutes, and the landscape changed. It was as though a brick had just hit my windshield, my head jerked back in such shock. As though the tornado's path had known where one sidewalk ended and the next one began, everything went from being undamaged to utterly destroyed. Within five feet of the perfectly erect buildings on one side of the street, similar buildings were destroyed and left in piles of rubble on the other side. Nothing was left standing as far as I could see. There were no buildings, no houses, and no gas stations. Where trees had once stood, casting pools of welcoming shade in the yards of homes and shops, there were jagged broken branches, foot-high trunks, and nothingness. It was difficult to wrap my mind around how people had even survived the force that could do this to solid structures and stately trees.

I couldn't believe what I was seeing. As I drove a few more minutes, it hit me. I turned my car around and drove down the same road. I needed to take it in again. Home Depot was now just a large white tent. Without a wall and half of its ceiling, you could see all the way through Academy Sports and Outdoors. Despite the wasteland that was now Joplin, Missouri, its residents weren't filled with despair. There was hope, triumph, and encouragement in people's eyes. They were starting to heal.

You don't have to go to the scene of a natural disaster to experience the blessing of giving to others. Whether it's volunteering at your child's school, serving food at a local homeless shelter, or educating someone on the very real problem of human trafficking, put time in your schedule to give back. Find a way to help someone else. We all say, "I need to give more." Stop just saying it. Put it on your calendar. Make it a weekly or bi-monthly activity. Get your spouse and kids involved. It's a great way to teach children selflessness and thankfulness.

It gives you the opportunity to learn from others. It opens your mind and gives you a new appreciation for all that you've been given in your life. So many people, places, and organizations need you. I know you are busy. We all are busy. I know you have trouble finding five minutes in your day for you. But if you put it on the calendar as you would a meeting, it becomes part of your schedule. It's something you do every third Wednesday of the month or every Sunday after church.

Don't think disasters, difficulties, and tragedies can't happen to you. We all need help. If you were stranded, broke, homeless, jobless, or abandoned, wouldn't you want someone, anyone to step up and offer to help? Wouldn't you want to know that someone cares about you? Stop thinking, *Someone else will do it.* No, YOU need to do it! Stop believing, *I don't have time.* You have time to get your hair or nails done, go to lunch with friends, or a movie. So, yes, you do have time. You have all the time it takes, because you can give as little or as much as you want.

Get your girlfriends together or start a girlfriend group. Make it the first Monday of every month event, where your girlfriends all bond and catch up over two hours at the local shelter or soup kitchen. Volunteer for the Society of Women Who Love Shoes (not just for girls), whose slogan is "Healing one sole at a time" by helping those affected by domestic violence.

Whether it's an hour a week or two hours a month, there is no amount of time that's too small to give. Imagine what you can achieve when you pay it forward. The world can change. When you volunteer, you're not only helping others; you are helping yourself. You are learning about yourself and allowing yourself to grow. Never stop growing and learning. Start now to make a difference. The more people you get involved, the more lives you can change. How are you going to give back and how often? Who are you asking to get involved with you?

Make time in your monthly schedule to give and volunteer.

To laugh often and much, to win the respect of intelligent people and the affection of children, to earn the appreciation of honest critics and endure the betrayal of false friends, to appreciate beauty, to find the best in others, to leave the world a bit better, whether by a healthy child, a garden patch...to know even one life has breathed easier because you have lived. This is to have succeeded!

—Ralph Waldo Emerson

CHAPTER 40: *Dinnertime*

Being busy is not an excuse to let things slide. If that were the case, people wouldn't get anything done or ever spend time on things that matter. When something is important, you find time to make it happen. Put simply, you prioritize.

Dinnertime has somehow lost its value in many families. It's no longer a time for connecting with one another. Everyone goes their separate ways and eats on the run.

Maria Shriver told a story about dinner in her family when she was a child. Each child was required to come to the table prepared to talk about what they did that day, both their successes and failures. They had to come to the table with ideas of what they would accomplish the next day and how they would do it. Those moments remained with her and taught her responsibility, and they helped her reach her goals.

What is dinnertime like in your house? Is your daughter on the phone in her room? Is your son playing video games? Are you texting? The last meal of the day should be spent around a table. There should be no television on or phones allowed at the table. This time is just for the family. It gives your family a chance to get together to recall your day, tell what happened, discuss how to resolve issues, or plan what lies ahead for the family.

Hold yourself accountable too. If the phone rings, don't jump up to get it. Let it go to voicemail. If it's important, the caller will leave a message. To me, there is nothing worse than having a meal with someone who interrupts the time we're sharing together to pick up their phone and answer a call that could wait. It tells the person they are with that the call is more important than she is. Emergencies arise, and if that's the case, excuse yourself and step outside to answer your phone. Don't sit at the table, whether you are at a restaurant or at home, and talk on the phone. It's rude.

Dinnertime is the time for you to come together as a family, not be divided. If you are separate at that special time of the day, what does that say about the rest of your life? If you are unable to come together as a family at one point in the day, then where do your priorities really lie?

I realize that sometimes things come up and you can't always be together for every dinnertime. Maybe your spouse works second shift or you have a business meeting at night. Then get together for breakfast. Make it a point to schedule time for the family to eat together at least once every day. You don't want to be so absent from one another's lives that you don't know what is going on with everyone.

Make it a priority to set aside time for dinner. You might have to eat earlier or later than usual. If you set this time aside for each other, you will have a stronger bond and connection with the people who matter most in your life. Do it on a regular basis, not just once a month, you will be glad you do.

If you don't hold yourself accountable, you can't hold someone else accountable. Make sure you are playing by the rules too. It will make dinner a pleasant time of day, and one you will look forward to—and maybe your family will too.

More importantly, it is a time where you come together as a family...a unified group...knowing no one in this world would ever replace the bond you share. You know that no matter what happens, you are *family*. So be sure to make dinnertime a special part of the day set aside just for those who matter most in life. You will always remember those moments.

Dinnertime is for coming together to share the day as a unified group.

This is my **wish**
for you:

             comfort
                on difficult days,

smiles
when sadness intrudes,

             laughter
                to kiss your lips,

rainbows to follow
the clouds,

         sunsets
           to warm your heart,

           friendships
            to brighten your being,

hugs
when spirits sag,

beauty
for your eyes to see,

Patience to
accept the truth

faith
so that you can believe,

courage to
know yourself,

confidence
for when you doubt,

love
to complete your life.

—Anonymous

The Power Of...

1. *Attitude*

For the longest time, I never knew what they were. It never occurred to me that these two things could literally change my life. Sometimes this realization comes in the wake of a moment and other times it builds slowly. No matter the case, there is absolutely no denying it: The most important things in your life are your attitude and perspective. You might argue that you can't live without love, and yes, you need money to pay the bills. You may say your kids are the most important part of your life. But you may find a constant, burning desire to truly *live* the life you somehow know you were meant to live. You may long to follow your dreams.

Your attitude is the one thing that gets you through life. Your attitude about love allows you to think you can't live without it. You attitude about work helps you to find a job where you can earn enough to pay the bills. If you have a hunger for success, that probably compels you to work harder to have leisure money. Your attitude about kids—having them, caring for them, and loving them makes you believe they are the most important part of your life. Everything stems from your attitude about life, love, responsibility, finances, people, and most of all yourself.

Over four years had passed, and I was still at the same job. Every time I walked through the doors, I felt like my soul was dying. Do you have a job like that? I somehow managed, day after day, to put one foot in front of the other and make my way through the door, only to be tortured the whole time I was there. The boss was disrespectful and did not in any way know how to treat her employees. She yelled and snapped at us on a daily basis, rolling her eyes at something she didn't like. Imagine working at a place where your boss cussed at you and thought nothing of it. She would sit in her office and pour herself glasses of wine as though this behavior was the norm. She put each of us down as easily as she talked bad about other employees in front of their peers. She had no ethics or moral values, yet she was in charge of a fine dining establishment. We felt we had no recourse, because she directly affected our pay. She dictated our stations, the number of tables we waited on, and how many people would be seated at those tables. She controlled our financial intake, and she knew it. I thought about going to her boss several times, but I knew the result would be the same. He would talk to her, but she ultimately controlled all the money I made. I just hated the thought of starting a new job somewhere else because I was only working there until my career took off. But eventually I realized that no amount of money is worth such demoralizing behavior from a boss.

When I came back to work from spending twelve days in Europe, I was told that my boss had been telling another employee things I had supposedly said that I hadn't. She was telling outright lies about me. That was it. I didn't deserve this. I was one of her top employees, and this was how she chose to treat me. I'd had enough and put my two-week notice in.

My boss was not working that day, but the next day I confronted her about it. I told her she intentionally created a hostile work environment, because my co-worker had believed her lies, become furious, and yelled at me. That's how I found out about it in the first place. She admitted to saying it and even said that she should never have said anything, but it was too late. She had created the hostility, and she was the general manager of the place.

When I put my two-week notice in the night before, I had no idea what I was going to do next. I didn't have another job lined up. I hadn't even thought about quitting. It was an emotional (yes, I admit it) and a spontaneous decision, but I was done. I was finished allowing the bosses to treat me that way. They disrespected the employees because they felt they could do it and suffer no consequences. I was finished giving them permission to treat me worse than my family, friends, or even strangers treat me. The longer they kept doing it, the more they thought they could. Enough was enough. I knew I deserved better than that. I took back my power...the power I never should have given away.

After all the time and energy I put into that place, I was sad the way things ended, but I wasn't sad I left. On my last day, it didn't really sink in that I had quit my job. That actually happened two days later at a time when I would normally have been getting ready for work. I felt so...free. I was released from all the drama, negativity, and backstabbing. I had always known I was imprisoned in that work environment. I just didn't realize I had actually been in solitary confinement.

As the days passed, I knew that was the best decision I could have made. I released myself from the pain and torment of continuing to live that life. My boss actually did me a favor by showing her true colors, because it allowed me permission to get out of that place. I had thought about leaving several times because I knew I deserved better. I was always working toward my dreams, so in my mind, the job was only temporary. I never would have thought that "temporary" would turn into four years.

Once I left, it was as though I was seeing the world with new eyes for the first time in years. I started going to networking events. I had forgotten that most people are actually nice, encouraging, and positive. They build you up and want you to succeed. I had forgotten to surround myself with those people...like-minded people. I have always been full of energy and optimism, and somehow I allowed those negative co-workers to affect my attitude and thereby control me. I never knew that my attitude about that job poured into other aspects of my life. Whether it was in my interactions with customer service agents or family members, I became a little more quick-tempered and curt, and that isn't me.

When you surround yourself with upbeat, positive people, opportunities present themselves. I became open and willing to respond to whatever came my way. I wanted to move in another direction, and I followed the ways that appeared. When you change your attitude about things (work, responsibility, money, to name a few), new opportunities open before you and you finally see another world—one that was there all along, but you just forgot to look. Don't allow yourself to get so caught up in what you are doing or what you think you should be doing that you forget to look at the other doors opening around you. Where you think you need to go may not be the right direction for you. Don't have tunnel vision; otherwise, you might pass by other paths without giving them a chance. They may be exactly what you've been looking for, and what you're meant to do.

When your attitude alters, so does your perspective. Changing your perspective isn't always easy. At that old job, there was a time when I would look at what others had earned that day and I would want to make that amount too. It took me a while to get to the point where I was grateful for what I had earned. Someone was always making less than I was. I changed my perspective and again things came my way.

After I left that job, I gave myself time to figure out my next step. It was refreshing not to have to go to a job I hated. My perspective on life completely changed. I finally had time to play volleyball, meet new friends, and network with other likeminded professionals. I felt like the world was my canvas, and I could literally do anything.

Each day was a new adventure. That's when I started writing my first book. I always knew I loved writing, but I didn't know how much until I began writing my book. During this process, I researched the possibility of writing articles for newspapers and magazines. After I decided to take my career in that direction, something was still bothering me. I wanted to have a direct impact on helping people. Yes, people would read my work, but being physically in front of people, talking with them and being able to look into their eyes, was different. That's when I knew I was going to be a speaker and consultant. My talk show had allowed me to do it, and I just felt it—that I still wanted to help people.

If not for quickly quitting my job and not having a Plan B, I don't know if speaking and coaching would have ever occurred to me, but it came to me because my perspective on life had altered.

Life is always and only a matter of perspective. Tweak your perspective. Stand at a different angle, and you will see that life is so much better, more fulfilling, and more fun than you first saw. Alter your perspective, and you will see it from someone else's standpoint. You will know he is hurt and doesn't know how to tell you. Change your perspective, and you will realize it's not that big of a deal; there is no need to yell, and money comes and goes.

Take a moment to consider your own attitude; are you positive? Upbeat? Negative? Unsupportive? Are you a Debbie Downer or a Positive Polly? Do you have a can-do attitude? How does your attitude affect your daily life? How does it affect others? How do you treat others based on your attitude about what they do/don't do, how much money they make, or who you believe them to be? How does your attitude rub off on other people? How do they respond to it?

When I was a teenager, my mom used to say, "It's not what you say; it's how you say it." I hated that saying and thought, *That is the stupidest saying ever.*

I never really understood what it meant until I became an adult. But it's true (don't tell my mom). It's not what you say. It's how you say it. Think of receiving a $10,000 bonus. How would you say "hi" to the first person you see after receiving such good news? Now think of getting in a seven-car pileup on the highway, and it was your fault. How would you say "hi" to the first person you see? Your attitude is affected by what occurred before seeing that person, but it doesn't have to be. You control your attitude, just like you control everything else about you. You have the ability to adjust your attitude in every situation, just like you can your perspective. The seven-car pileup happened to me. Yes, I was really upset about it, but I focused (or rather, I put my perspective) on the fact that no one was hurt in it.

Remember, it's always and only a matter of perspective and attitude. Be willing to adjust yours, and others will be willing to do the same for you. When it seems that everyone you meet is negative, maybe they are simply reacting to *your* attitude. When you alter your mindset and your attitude, your whole world changes, thereby changing everyone around you, too, and allowing you to view everything with new eyes.

> # Change your attitude and perspective and witness how your world changes, too.

Live with intention.
Walk to the edge.
Listen Hard. **Practice**
wellness. **Play** with
abandon. **Laugh.**
Choose with **no** regret.
Continue to **learn.**
Appreciate your **friends.**
Do what you **love.**
Live as if this is
all there is.

—Mary Anne Radmacher

2. Positive Thinking

Are you familiar with the book called *The Secret*, which is about the forces of the universe, also known as the law of attraction? Its basic premise is this: What you put out to the word is what you will get back. When you constantly release negativity, the "why me" attitude or the "of course this is what happens to me" mentality, that is exactly what will boomerang back to you. How are negative thoughts affecting your life and keeping you from living the life you love?

It was at a fundraising event where they were raffling off prizes. Cecilia hadn't won anything, and all the prizes were almost gone. She finally looked at the guy calling the new number. She made eye contact with him before he announced the number he had just drawn. He said, "The last three numbers are…"

Cecelia stared at him, wanting him to call her number. She mouthed "three."

He said, "Three."

Then she mouthed "one," as she continued to look directly at him.

He said, "One."

Then, as though she knew he was going to say, "Three," she mouthed "three" as she looked into his eyes, willing him to say her last number.

He said, "Three."

She stood up, excitement igniting inside of her, and called out, "That's me!"

The power of positive thinking will win every time.

It's as though the universe is working with you and not against you when you think positively. You have to *know*, not just believe, but absolutely know that it's going to happen, just like you know you are going to get out of bed each day. You may wake up at a different time on Saturday than you do on Tuesday, but you know you will get up.

The power of positive thinking is like a magnet that pulls the desired result to you with tremendous force. You are putting your desires out to the world, and the universe will conspire to make them happen. When you think positively, you follow up that thinking with likeminded actions. You won't allow anyone or anything to stand in the way of fulfilling your dreams. When you know it will happen, you will act accordingly. Do whatever is necessary to make it happen, whether it's making phone calls, meeting new clients, or prioritizing your life.

The opposite is also true. When you think the world is conspiring against you and things aren't going your way, you will start to respond accordingly. You won't put forth as much time, you will procrastinate, or you will constantly find excuses for why you "can't" do something or why something won't work. You will stop putting forth any efforts, thinking it won't happen for you anyway, so "why bother?" Why keep putting money toward it? Why keep looking for the man of your dreams? Why go after the job you really want? You tell yourself that dreams only happen to other people, not you.

If you have this defeatist attitude, you will be right. The things you want most in life won't happen for you, because your thoughts are barriers to their existence. You are allowing your thoughts to keep you from achieving your goals and being who you are meant to be. Since actions follow thoughts, you will never act on the dreams you want, because your thoughts are stopping you before you can start.

How do you get out of this rut? Change your thinking. Stop believing the world is against you. Stop thinking, "Why me?" or

"This only happens to me." We all go through tough times, but it's only temporary. You have the strength to not only get through it, but to thrive in the midst of challenges. You have the power to make your life better, more fulfilling. You know when bad or negative things happen, you will come out the other side stronger, more determined, and more alive than before. You will persevere. You have the power to change your life, but first you must alter your thinking. Only allow positive, uplifting, encouraging thoughts to enter you mind. When the opposite pokes their way through, push them out again. You don't have the time or energy for them. They have no control over you and your life. You only have time for the good in life, which comes through a positive mindset. You will soon experience the power of positive thoughts, and how they can change your whole world.

> What you put out to the world is what you will receive. This is the power of your thoughts.

Take pride
in how far
you have come,
and have **faith** in
how far you can go!

—Christian Larson

3. Believing In Yourself—Self-Confidence

Many children naturally have a high level of self-confidence. Some excel at sports or in school. Others rely on beauty, charm, wittiness, goofiness, or some other personality trait. When people compliment you enough when you are young, you believe what they say. If enough people tell you, "You are funny," or "You are so talented," you start to think it. When you score enough goals in soccer or receive a lot of As in school, you know you are a good player or student. When others tell you this, especially the adults in your life, it gets reiterated.

Many of us lose sight of our natural abilities and self-confidence as adults. Life beats us down and we forget who we are. Most of us aren't competing in sports or for good grades. We aren't usually performing in a band or goofing around at school cracking jokes. When you're an adult and your confidence begins to lag, where do you go to restore it? How do you build it?

You may be hearing the same thing for so long that you start to believe it. "You need to lose weight," "Why don't you do something with yourself," or "You can't be that stupid." The negative comments don't even have to be that direct to be hurtful. It can be something as simple as someone telling you, "If you had done such and such, then..." This can take on several iterations: If you had taken this route instead of the route you took, we wouldn't be late...If you had cooked the chicken for 20 minutes instead of 25, it wouldn't be dry...If you had done what I told you instead of what *you* did, then none of this would have happened...

When someone criticizes you continually, you start to think you can't do anything right. If that person knows the "best" way to do everything, then why doesn't he do it instead? If you constantly hear how you don't measure up (that's how it translates in your mind), you believe you aren't good enough. You buy into what that person says, especially if it's a family member, spouse, or close friend.

Over time, this tears apart your self-esteem and self-confidence. You believe you can't do anything right. It doesn't matter if it's related to what you get torn down about. For example, if someone tells you over and over how bad your cooking is, then you might think that you can't clean the house the "right" way either. Or if she tells you constantly that you shouldn't let your kids eat cookies, then you might start to think that you don't know what's best for your kids. Sometimes we think of it as merely nagging, but it hurts us to the point of destruction. It starts weighing on our self-confidence and causes us to doubt our abilities to accomplish any task adequately.

Then it breaks down our self-esteem and self-respect. We think we don't deserve things. This devastation affects not only how we see ourselves but also how we view the world, which alters our perspective. After years of hearing this negativity, you are so broken; you don't know how to rebuild.

You can do and achieve anything and everything you want to no matter what anyone else may say. Your self-confidence plays a vital role in everything you do from the way you dress and walk to your posture and the way you talk to someone else. It may keep you from or help you get a job, a spouse, and respect. It can make you a better or worse parent. Just like self-confidence, your self-esteem alters your view of yourself and the world. It allows you to think you don't deserve a spouse (or a better one), the job you want, or to be treated fairly. You may hide your feelings so others don't know the pain you're struggling with, or you may become depressed, not knowing how to help yourself.

Beginning to believe in yourself isn't hard to do. Look at yourself in the mirror every day. Really look, every day, and by this I mean, take a good long look into your eyes. You already do it, whether you're brushing your teeth, styling your hair, or applying make-up. Look at yourself before you begin your routine. Starting today, make this part of your daily ritual, first thing when you get up in the morning. Before you make breakfast for yourself or the family, before you shower, and yes, before you even go to the bathroom, look at yourself in the mirror—wild hair, bad breath, mouth guard and all.

Take a good, long, hard look at you. See the freckles. Look at the red patch. Really examine the laugh lines. Try to figure out which one came from where. Trace the scars with your index finger. Smooth your ring finger across the bags under your eyes and think, *I need to put some cucumbers on these.* Appreciate your strong jaw, cleft chin, or your olive skin.

None of us can compare ourselves to others. We all know there will always be someone younger, richer, smarter, prettier, funnier, more talented, and faster than we are. For every one thing that person has above you, you have something above them. Maybe you're more caring, genuine, loving, and happier than they are. Did you ever think about that?

If we go through life comparing ourselves to other people, we will never be happy with whom we are, which will keep us from ever being happy in life. We will constantly be criticizing ourselves, finding fault in whom we are, and scrutinizing everything we do. Too many people out there will do this to us, so we shouldn't treat ourselves so harshly. You don't need to do that to yourself. You don't judge others; why are you judging yourself? Holding yourself to higher standards than you hold others is unhealthy. It only hurts you in your quest. You need to see all the greatness you have and all the qualities you bring to the world. No one out there is exactly like you. You have a magic that is all yours. Own it! Embrace it! Love it! Thank you for being you...exactly who you are!

See yourself through new eyes or in a different way. Each day you will pick out one new thing you like about yourself. You can be very specific. It can be how your eyes change colors depending on what you wear, the freckle you have in the middle of your back, or how you are double jointed. Maybe it is the cellulite on your thighs or that when you stand, your knees don't touch when your feet do. You may love the fineness of your hair, or even that you don't have any left after chemotherapy caused you to lose it all. Your beauty marks may be the scar from your three C-sections or the baseball sized skin graph on your arm after the car wreck surgery. It may be the stint in your chest from dialysis or the muscles in your arms from rolling your wheelchair.

Look in the mirror each day and see yourself again for the first time. What do you really see? What do you like? What do you love? You have so many redeeming features...so many lovable parts. So, tell me, what are they? Go grab a mirror and pick one right now for me. What is it? Call your best friend and tell her what hers is, and ask her what yours is. Then tell her what you think yours is. Do they match? You have so many attributes that you don't even know you have that add character to who you are...that give you strength and wisdom and that tell a story. I want to hear that story. I want you to know you are worth it. You are beautiful exactly how you are, exactly who you are, flaws and all. You are so precious! You are admirable, intelligent, and courageous. So, what is your best feature today, and what is its story?

You can put yourself on the shelf—your dreams, desires, future, wants, relationships, finances, and passions—but remember, as long as you do this, you will never be the person you are meant to be. You will never reach your potential. Wouldn't it be better to take yourself down off that shelf and focus on you for a change?

Believe in YOU. Doors will fly open for you!

What Else Can Help Self-Confidence?

How can the act of getting dressed increase your self-confidence? We are all insecure about something. It might be your glasses, weight, or hair. It could be your height, shoe size, or facial features. There are things that you can change and others you can't. Learn to know and accept the difference.

There are days I don't feel I look good and other days when I look in the mirror and think, *Wow, your hair looks great*, or, *That blue shirt brings out your eyes*.

One way for you to feel better about yourself is to dress to impress. Women tend to dress depending on their moods for that day. You might want to wear an off the shoulder shirt to feel a bit sexier. Or if you are running errands, jeans will suffice. If you want to increase your self-confidence, dress accordingly. If you are feeling down, don't dress like you are. Put on heels and a cute top; find something that's going to lift your spirits. Dressing in sweats is just going to keep you in the dumps, and your mood will only get worse. Not only do you feel down, but now you *look* like you feel that way. When you look good, you feel good. There is nothing good feeling about a no make-up, sweat pants-wearing, frumpy–lady day.

If you don't have makeup on, do you feel a little less than your usual self? Does your attitude shift just a bit? Are you not quite as confident or sure of yourself? It's as though make-up might give you that extra boost. Even if you put on powder and mascara, you would feel better about yourself. In feeling more attractive, your self-confidence increases.

When you are running errands, don't just throw on a t-shirt and jeans. I'm not saying you need to grocery shop all decked out in heels, with full make-up on and your hair done to the nines. Look the way you want to feel. Wear a nice button-down shirt and flats. Make sure your hair is brushed. You never know whom you might see or meet at the store. You don't want to look like you just rolled out of bed. Dress to impress, even if you don't think you will see anyone worth impressing. You are dressing for yourself, because even when walking through the grocery store, you will know you are the best looking, best-dressed person there. Now that's a way to increase your self-confidence.

> # Dress to impress and your self-confidence will increase.

too often we underestimate
the power of a touch, a smile,
a kind word, a listening ear,
an honest compliment,
or the smallest act of caring,
all of which have the potential
to turn a life around.

—Leo Buscaglia

4. One

You are one. You are only one. But you are one. It only takes one person to start a revolution, begin a foundation, ignite a nation, have a dream, or change the world. You are only one person. But you are one.

"I'm only one person, Jessica, what can I do?" It took one person to invent the light bulb.

"Jessica, I don't know the first thing about starting a non-profit." What causes do you care about? It took one person, Nancy Brinker, to start a breast-cancer awareness foundation in honor of her sister, Susan G. Komen. She has raised over 1.4 billion dollars and helped millions.

You are only one person, but you are one. It all begins with one person. Yes, you may have to ask for help. You might need others to handle the business aspect while you are in charge of creative. You may have to work longer hours, try things that have never been done before, or beg others for their assistance. You will have to fight for what you believe in, stand up against critics, and persevere when there is little money. You can do it! You have everything within you to make a difference. Everything you need to succeed is inside you. Dig deep. Never give up. Don't listen to others who say it's hard, it can't be done, or how long it will take. Ignore them. They haven't wanted anything as badly as you want this.

You might not set out to change the world...but you will change the world for one person. And that's success. What are the possibilities when you put your mind to something? What can you achieve when you give it your all? Have you thought of a new effective way for people to find each other? Are you the next Nancy Brinker, changing the face of a disease? Do you have the compassion of Oprah? What will you accomplish when you set your mind and heart to do it?

Will you start a movement? Are you going to find a greener way? Do you build a non-profit daycare for teenage moms so that they can finish school knowing their children are taken care of safely? What are you doing in your life to help others? How are you getting out of your comfort zone and showing the world how one person can make a difference?

It's more than just about you. You are speaking for others who can't speak for themselves, maybe because they feel as though their subject is still taboo, and so they are too embarrassed, ashamed, or humiliated to speak up. Maybe they don't have the resources you have. You are their voice. Speak, speak, speak, and never shut up! Give them what they cannot give themselves. Help them beyond what they and you thought was possible. Find a way to open the doors to opportunity so that they, in return, can help so many others in a similar situation.

None of us is alone in our struggles. Someone else is going through something similar. Someone else doesn't know what to do or where to go. She doesn't have the support and love to trudge through it. She feels alone and helpless. Let her know she is needed in this world. She exists…she matters! Show her you are there for her no matter what. Even if you don't know her, reach out your hand, stretch your heart, and light the way for her. Guide her to her future. You don't have to set out to change the world, but you never know—you just might. When you change her world, you change the world of so many others.

You are one. You are but just one. But you are one. It only takes one. It all begins with you. You are one! And the power of one can change the world. So, whether it's for one or for many, how are you changing the world today?

The power of one…it all begins with you!

open your eyes
to the beauty around you,

open your mind
to the wonders of life,

open your heart
to those who love you,

and always
be true to yourself.

–Donna Davis

5. *You*

Be yourself. Don't have qualms about or make excuses for who you are. Embrace it! I encourage you to find out who you are, accept who you are, and love who you are. There is a magic to you that's yours alone. Own it. No one else has the same special combination of personality, humor, looks, intelligence, sparkle, joy, and love. You cannot be duplicated. You are unique. Love it and Love YOU! You are destined for GREATNESS.

I was volunteering at a detention center for girls, and we were breaking into groups. One girl raised her hand and said, "I want to be with her," as she pointed toward me.

I thought, *Well, I guess that's a compliment*, but I didn't really understand why she wanted to be with me. I had probably only said about three words so far. I hadn't "done" anything in my mind for her to want to be with me.

I relayed this to my best friend, Matt, later that same day, and he very quickly interrupted me and said, "She is seeing you. She sees your light."

He said, "There is a light that shines in and through you that other people see. They want to be a part of that. They want to have more of that. They are drawn to you."

Matt was saying you don't have to "try" to do anything for someone to like you. You don't need to "try" to be any way for someone to be attracted to you and your presence.

The following day, I had a mastermind session with three other people. We each introduced our background and ourselves, and then took about ten minutes to ask questions to the group. When it was my turn, we talked about my blog. The other lady said to me, "You have an energy that people are drawn to. You pull people in, and they want to have more of you."

As I took in and processed what she was saying, she continued, "Doing a video blog, instead of just a written blog, would be beneficial, because people are intrigued and interested in you, and your energy shines through when you speak."

As soon as this lady started talking, I immediately thought of the conversation I'd had the day before with Matt. It was as though I was being hit over the head with a brick. Okay, I got it! Yet, had I not had that talk with Matt, I may not have received the message so readily.

You don't have to be anyone or anything you are not. All you have to be is yourself. Don't try to be funny or profound. People want to know you so they can like you for who you really are. When you are exactly who you are, faults and all, that's when success will find you. When you "try" to be someone or something else, you will not feel whole. Something will be missing, because you will be lying to others by pretending to be someone other than yourself.

When you are being who you truly are, energy will ignite within you. You will possess a passion and a love for not only others but for yourself. You won't have to utter a single word or do anything for people to notice. Whether you stand in one place or walk into a room, people will be drawn and attracted to you. You may not be able to put your finger on why this happens. It will be something you can't control. You may not see it yourself, but you will definitely feel it. It is your energy, your aura, and your presence... The light will shine in and through you in all that you do.

> # Don't be anyone you aren't...
> # let people see your true light.

GO INTO THE WORLD AND DO WELL. BUT MORE IMPORTANTLY, GO INTO THE WORLD AND DO GOOD.

—MINOR MYERS JR.

Conclusion

What are you doing to make sure you are living your greatest life? What could you be doing better? Differently? With more enthusiasm? Life isn't easy. Things get in the way, but stop making excuses. People who started with far less than you have are succeeding. You can too!

My wish for you is that through this book you have learned something about your life, your future, and yourself. It is my hope that you will go further than you ever thought possible. Let this book serve as a springboard for launching you into your new life. You may not yet be able to envision the plan that's in store for your life, but have faith and *know* it exists. You are on the right path toward living your greatest life. You are destined for greatness!

I believe in you, and I know you can and will take the steps to make it happen. You have everything within you to make it possible. Thank you for taking this journey with me. I would love to hear your journey, so please don't hesitate to share it with me. Enjoy life to the fullest.

Since we were kids, my mom has cross-stitched gifts, framed pictures, sayings, and pillows for us. I still have several around my house. My mom is very talented with handcrafts. About seven years ago, she cross-stitched a Christmas gift for me, and at the time, I was skeptical about it because I can be a bit picky in what I like and dislike. But when Jasmine told me that I would like the gift, I knew I would. I just didn't realize that to this day it would be one of my favorite gifts of all time.

My mom had cross-stitched the saying, "Live the life you love. Don't settle for less. Laugh often. Believe." Above the words she had stitched some beautiful, colorful butterflies. The saying is perfect for me, because those who know me would call it my mantra for life.

If you allow yourself to be your authentic self, the life you want will find you. If you lose your way, turn to this book like a trusted friend to help you get back on track. Hold tight to who you are, never thinking you deserve less. Never let someone else think that about you, either, and never believe them when they say, "Well, your standards are too high." Just because their standards aren't doesn't mean you should lower yours. Don't accept that.

You know who you are. Enjoy the moments. You can never laugh too much, and make sure you laugh at yourself, too. Even when things are difficult in life, laugh. Through the sadness and pain, laugh.

In all times, good or bad, success or failure, love or loss, believe. Believe things will get better...believe there is greatness in you... believe in your future...believe in your life... believe in yourself. Never stop believing in all you are, all you have to give, and all that is to come your way.

If you live by a similar mantra as what my mom cross-stitched for me, your heart will always guide you in your life. No matter if it says, "Speak out," "Walk away," "Just do it," or "Give and you will get," listen to your heart. It will never lead you astray.

I see you. I hear you. What you say and who you are matters. You make a difference. You matter. Who you are means something to friends, your parents, kids, and me. When talking to someone, especially when you disagree with her, say, "I hear you." You are still being true to yourself, even if you think you are "right" in the situation. People want to be heard, and when you say this, you allow her to know that what she says is important and it matters. She matters—her thoughts, her words, and her actions. Yes, she matters.

You are worthy to have the life you are meant to live. Know you are worthy enough for happiness, love, and respect. You are worthy of greatness! You are worthy of everything good that is coming your way. You are alive, so you are worthy. You are enough, exactly as you are.

Never give up on yourself and all you are. You are destined for so much goodness. Realize your greatness.

As I part with you, I will leave you with one last thought.

Things weren't going quite as I had planned. Then again, that's life. I was still waiting tables, trying to get my career off the ground. I was making headway, but not as much as I wanted. Then one day my friend Lacy told me how she used me as an example of success to her sister. I said, "Success? Me? Why do you say that?" I had never seen myself as a success. In my mind, success had always been closely tied with financial stability. Waiting tables did not signify financial stability…at least to my purpose and me.

Lacy said, "I was telling her that I have always seen you as a success even though things haven't always worked out the way you planned. You hate waiting tables and wish that something had panned out better than it has, but…"

I interrupted her and said, "How have you seen me as a success when things haven't worked out as I planned?"

She continued, "You can never say you haven't seized every opportunity. You can never regret not going for something. All these things you have done are stepping stones leading to what will be God's plan in your life. You will be at the end of your life knowing that you tried your best. If you didn't, you would be full of regret."

Lacy said to think of it as a checklist. You are checking things off your list that you have discovered aren't your plan in life, and then you're on to the next venture.

Success is an internal game. It's more about what you think, feel, and believe than the resources at hand.

Lacy is right and knows me so well. I live life with no regrets, and living that way is not always easy. People will criticize. They won't understand. They will question what you are doing and your motives. But you MUST stay true to your path. In time, all will be revealed.

There are times that I question what I'm doing or a decision I'm about to make. If I'm ever unsure, I ask, "Will I regret not doing it?" If there is even a possibility or a small fraction of a chance the response is "Yes," then I have my real answer. I jump at the chance to do it.

You may be wondering, *Jessica, why don't you ask, 'Will I regret doing it?'* I know that my regret for not doing something is going to be higher than for doing it. I've never regretted doing something, but there have been plenty of times I've regretted *not* doing something. I don't want to live like that.

So, take a chance…risk something. If you don't, will you regret not doing it? Live life with no regrets and your life will be filled with so much joy, happiness, liberation, empowerment, and love.

The experience I had volunteering in Joplin with Lacy can't be duplicated. Every day for almost a week in one hundred-degree heat wearing long pants, face masks, and safety glasses, we carried debris from homes hoping in some small way to let those affected know that people cared about them. We heard stories of tragedy and survival, but I knew the human spirit trumped any disaster.

On our last day of volunteering, the bus was taking longer than normal to pick us up. Another volunteer asked if we wanted a ride back to the drop-off point. He was so kind; he allowed six of the volunteers, plus his three boys, to ride in his truck. Lacy, another volunteer, and I offered to ride in the back with his boys. As we rode down the streets, I was like a sponge, taking in every moment—the wind blowing in our hair, the broken trees, the shattered windows, unrecognizable buildings, and homes where you think no one could have survived yet they did. In that moment, it was reiterated to me: it's not about how many possessions we have, what kind, or how much they cost. It's about what we give to others and the legacy we leave behind when we are gone. I had someone take a picture of Lacy and me sitting on the edge of the truck bed, but no photo is as grand as the image in my mind or the memories of that week working in service to others alongside my best friend. That, my friend, is Living Your Greatest Life!

APPENDIX

Carlene Altom—Carlene's business website is http://CoreMSO. com. Or, you can go to coremso.blogspot.com and subscribe to receive daily email updates of Carlene's words of wisdom and advice.

Meredith Creek—Meredith practices at 4030 Mount Carmel Tobasco Road, Suite 102, Cincinnati, Ohio 45255. Meredith's contact email is meredith.creek@gmail.com. You can also read Meredith's blog at http://thissideofthecreek.com or view her site www.meredithcreek.com, and you can find her in the resource *Psychology Today*.

Janee' Harrell—For more information about The Janee' Show, go to http://janeeharrell.com/.

Cindy L. Herb—To purchase Cindy's book, sign up for her newsletter, read her blog or find out more, please visit her website at http://JoyfulSurvivor.com.

Dianne Samoff—Want to attend an event, contribute, or keep informed with Dianne's Society of Women Who Love Shoes? Go to www.societyofwomenwholoveshoes.org.

ABOUT THE AUTHOR

Jessica jumps into life, and her mission is to help you leap in yours. After graduating from college, Jessica didn't know what career she wanted. She refused to settle in life, so she decided to search for her true passion, while going to grad school.

After graduating, she moved to Los Angeles, where she started her talk show The JessICAREctor Show. It thrived there for two years, before Jessica moved back to Texas to continue her show and get her third college degree in broadcast journalism.

Jessica knew she had found her passion by helping others in their lives. Whether it's through understanding, compassion, education, motivation, or perseverance, The JessICAREctor Show sets out to truly give everyone an opportunity to comprehend, learn, and support others through their stories. It has helped countless people and changed lives. It is seen worldwide at JessICAREctor.com and on youtube.com/JessICAREctor.

As a life coach, author, and speaker, Jessica's Live Your Greatest Life continues her mission of helping others. In order to be your authentic self, you must discover who you are and confront your fears. How do you do that? Where do you even start? Jessica strives for you to take the necessary steps to live the life you've always dreamed. You are destined for GREATNESS! There is nothing holding you back but you. So now is the time to Live Your Greatest Life!

Live Your Greatest Life is Jessica's first published book. She is currently writing her second book in the Live Your Greatest Life series. Jessica is also the author of another book series about where to find "the one," a city search for love, which guides you where to go, what to wear, and who you will find at specific places in major metropolitan areas.

Whether it's in Africa or Joplin, Jessica enjoys spending time volunteering. How can she help you?

JessICAREctor Productions LLC was formed in 2009 and was featured in Cambridge Who's Who in 2009 and 2010.

Jessica is single and resides in the Dallas/Fort Worth, Texas Metroplex. To learn more about Jessica, her coaching, and her books, or to schedule her for speaking engagements, please visit www.JessICAREctor.com or email her at Jessica@JessICAREctor.com.

Find Jessica on social media at facebook.com/liveyourgreatestlifetoo, facebook.com/liveyourgreatestlifebook, and twitter.com/jessicarector.

So you have heard the term, life coach, but what does it really mean? More importantly, what does it mean to you?

A life coach helps you to achieve a better future. Jessica will guide you to be who you are meant to be and reach your potential. She delivers a very hands-on approach, going through the individual steps to help you progress in life while tackling a variety of issues that may be holding you back. She walks alongside you with no judgment, allowing you to feel comfortable revealing your secrets in order to move forward. She wants you to succeed as much as you want to succeed. She will support, understand, and encourage you, but she will also hold you accountable in your journey. Her mission is for you to live your greatest life.

You don't have to live in the same area as Jessica for her coaching services. With email and Skype, coaching can be done from anywhere in the world. Contact her at Jessica@JessICAREctor.com today to book your free 30-minute consultation.

Made in the USA
Charleston, SC
24 April 2012